AK SING RUN WRITE PETE FIGHT CARE

LISTEN SCORE CLIMB WORK PER

RUN WRITE DREAM COMPETE FIGHT CARE CHANGE ACT

ISTEN SCORE SURVIVE CLIMB SKATE WORK PERFORM

T SURVIVE SKATE WORK PERFORM WONDER ACHIEVE

DREAM COMPETE FIGHT CARE CHANGE LOVE INNOVATE

RK PERFORM WONDER ACHIEVE DANCE TRANSFORM

WONDER ACHIEVE LEARN CREATE PLAY WIN LEAD ACT

E CLIMB SURVIVE SKATE ACT WORK PERFORM WONDER

RUN WRITE DREAM COMPETE FIGHT CARE CHANGE LOVE

CLIMB SURVIVE WONDER ACHIEVE DANCE TRANSFORM

ARE COMPETE SCORE CLIMB LISTEN LOVE INNOVATE

MB SURVIVE SKATE WIN LEAD SPEAK SING RUN WRITE

IDE INVENT DANCE TRANSFORM LISTEN SCORE CLIMB

CE TRANSFORM LISTEN SCORE CLIMB SURVIVE SKATE

WIN LEAD SPEAK ACT SING RUN WRITE LOVE INNOVATE

IG RUN WRITE DREAM COMPETE FIGHT CARE CHANGE

RAD

GIRLS

CAN

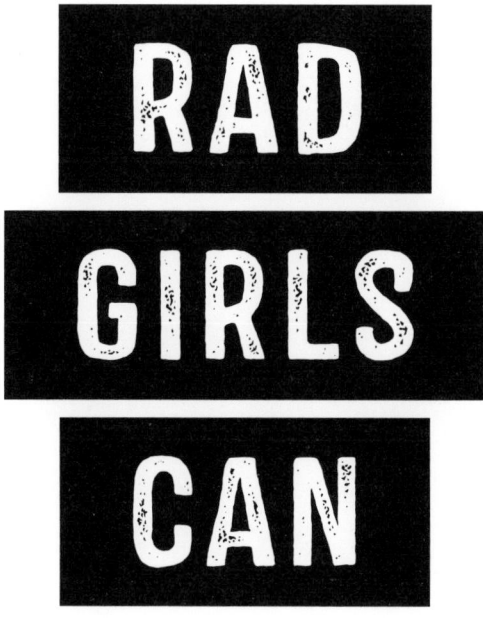

RAD GIRLS CAN

STORIES OF BOLD, BRAVE, AND BRILLIANT YOUNG WOMEN

Written by
KATE SCHATZ

Illustrated by
MIRIAM KLEIN STAHL

TEN SPEED PRESS
California | New York

Ten Speed Press and the Ten Speed Press colophon
are registered trademarks of Penguin Random House LLC.

Library of Congress Cataloging-in-Publication Data

Names: Schatz, Kate, author. | Klein Stahl, Miriam, illustrator.
   Title: Rad girls can : stories of bold, brave, and brilliant young women /
      Kate Schatz ; illustrated by Miriam Klein Stahl.
   Description: California : Ten Speed Press, 2018. | Includes bibliographical
      references and index.
   Identifiers: LCCN 2017049166
   Subjects: LCSH: Women—Biography. | Girls—Biography. | Women—History. |
      BISAC: BIOGRAPHY & AUTOBIOGRAPHY / Women. | SOCIAL SCIENCE / Women's
      Studies.
   Classification: LCC CT3205 .S38 2018 | DDC 920.72—dc23
   LC record available at https://lccn.loc.gov/2017049166

Hardcover ISBN: 978-0-399-58110-6
eBook ISBN: 978-0-399-58111-3

Printed in China

Design by Lizzie Allen

Running text font, Skopex Gothic, designed by Andrea Tinnes

10 9 8 7 6 5 4 3 2 1

First Edition

For all the rad kids—including our own.

For everyone who asked us, "Can you please
make your next book about girls?"

And for every girl who has stood up, spoken
out, taken a chance, tried something new,
followed a dream, and made the world a
better place—thank you!

CONTENTS

WELCOME TO
RAD GIRLS CAN

In this book, you'll find fifty stories about all *kinds* of girls and young women who've done incredible things—all before the age of twenty.

Some of the girls featured in this book are well-known, iconic figures: people like Anne Frank (page 38), Joan of Arc (page 90), and Helen Keller (page 85). But many of these girls may be unfamiliar to you, either because they're just beginning their rad journeys or because their stories haven't yet received the attention they deserve.

Most of the stories take place in the twentieth and twenty-first centuries, but there are a few girls profiled from the nineteenth century, like Mary Shelley (page 81) and Maria Mitchell (page 47), and several super-ancient stories (check out Khutulun, the Wrestling Princess, from the year 1260 on page 89). Some girls, like Misty Copeland (page 12), Ruby Bridges (page 64), and Janet Mock (page 51), are now grown-up, successful women. Their stories focus on the amazing things they did when they were younger, showing how they got to where they are today. And finally, many of these stories are about girls who are young *right now*, like author and activist Marley Dias (page 55), singer/songwriter Lorde (page 58), and pro rock climber Ashima Shiraishi (page 28).

Regardless of *when* these girls did great things, this book is mostly about *what* they did and *how* they did it. At some point in their lives, all of the girls in this book decided to *go for it*. They started fashion lines (see page 37), blogs (see page 25), and bands (see page 57). They stood up for their beliefs and challenged injustice in their schools (see page 67 and 72)—and in the federal courts (see page 21). They saw that something wasn't right—and they refused to be quiet about it.

The girls in these stories come from different backgrounds, cultures, and countries. Some have faced war, racism, poverty, and abuse, while others have lived safe, comfortable lives. Some helped shape laws, and some had to break the rules. Each girl in this book is as unique as her story—but they all share a sense of creativity, commitment, and courage. And they all *care*.

Some of these girls' accomplishments are *epic*. They get lead roles in movies (see page 53) and publish cool books (see page 79), and they win Nobel Prizes (see page 42) and gold medals (see page 19). But most change happens in small, incremental ways: one young person starts a hashtag on Twitter (see page 55), a girl learns about an unfair law (see page 25), a group of friends writes poetry about their experiences with discrimination (see page 33). It takes hard work, dedication, and patience to make a difference. But it also takes a first step, that initial spark to get you from wondering *Can I . . . ?* to realizing *I can!*

You can find rad girls *everywhere*: In the lab, in the classroom, in the ring, and in the pool. They're at the skate park, on the radio, and on the playground. They're playing on soccer fields and basketball courts. They're standing up at school and speaking out from the podium. They're gathering at marches and rallies, and they're connecting on the phone and online. And they're here, in these pages.

Do you know why we made this book? Because you asked us to. Okay, maybe you personally did not ask—but as Miriam and I traveled around the country visiting schools, classrooms, and libraries, telling stories about cool women from history, *a lot* of young people asked, "Can you *please* make a book about *girls*?" So we listened. This is for *you.*

MY OWN (RAD) STORY

When I was in sixth grade, I found a brand-new book at my local library: *50 Simple Things Kids Can Do to Save the Earth*. I can still remember flipping through the pages. I had never seen a book like that, aimed at someone like me. I read and reread it, learning about the many threats to our precious world, from greenhouse gases to the extinction of animals. I learned about recycling and saving water, and I felt empowered. I felt like I could actually do something.

The next time I went to the library, I picked up a pamphlet about animal rights from a big table covered with flyers and community announcements. It had a picture of a bunny on the cover, and it explained how a well-known cosmetics company was testing its makeup products on animals. Then I picked up another pamphlet that explained how a fast-food restaurant was cutting down rain forests in South America to make room for grazing cattle that would be turned into hamburgers. I had never really thought about where my food came from, or how the products I used were made. But suddenly, I was making connections.

That weekend I went to a sleepover birthday party for one of my best friends. A small group of us arrived, excited for a night of hot fudge sundaes and scary movies. As we hung out in the front yard, I shared with my friends—with great seriousness—what I'd learned; then I led our small group of girls in a "protest march" for the rain forests around the front yard. We did this for about five minutes, and I still remember the elated feeling of knowing I'd spoken out and taken a stand. Later I told my friends about the cosmetics company and animal testing, and how we should check to see if our shampoos and conditioners were cruelty-free. Then we made our hot fudge sundaes and got into our sleeping bags to watch scary movies.

Was our six-person boycott and tiny demonstration on a quiet suburban street a success? That depends on how you define success. My friends and I definitely didn't change the dangerous practices of massive corporations—but we *did* became aware of them. We spread the word to other friends. I didn't save the planet, but I *did* stick with my commitment to activism. I became a committed vegetarian. I kept reading books about the environment and activism. I sewed patches on my backpack, wore political T-shirts to school, and started writing poems, stories, and articles about politics, injustice, and feminism. I was definitely "that girl" who was always talking loudly about *some* issue. It didn't always make me super popular, but I was proud of myself.

Fast forward many years, and here I am, sharing this book with you. I'm still an activist, and now I'm an author, too. Would I be doing this work if I hadn't found *50 Simple Things Kids Can Do to Save the Earth* at the library? I can't say for sure, but I do know that such small discoveries have had an enormous impact on my life's journey. And each small action I took (challenging a friend who used an offensive slur, sharing an unpopular opinion during a classroom discussion, writing a poem that reflected a vulnerable truth) helped build my confidence as a girl—and then a woman— who wants to make the world a more just, peaceful place.

I hope the stories in this book inspire you to look at your community, your world, and yourself very closely. What do you see? What do you love? What might you want to improve—and how can you take action to make that happen?

In other words: how can *you* be rad?

A NOTE ON GENDER

This book focuses on girls and young women, including those who are transgender. We support the full rights and inclusion of young people of all gender identities. We also want to acknowledge that there are many rad young people who don't identify as male *or* female, boy *or* girl. They might be trans, or nonbinary, or they might just feel unsure as to where they fall on the gender spectrum. For many young people, gender is a shifting category that sometimes doesn't even feel relevant or important. That is all very real, and very okay.

We also acknowledge that there are *thousands* of stories about super rad boys and young men who've done wonderful, powerful things. We respect the boys who are working to make the world a better, more peaceful place, the boys who respect people of all genders and reject cultures of violence and misogyny. This is not always easy for boys, as gender roles and expectations can be just as challenging for boys as they are for girls, if not more so. We thank these boys, and we need them to keep up their important and often difficult work.

We believe in supporting the greatness of all young people, but we still feel it's important to highlight the efforts of girls. As I did the research for this book, I came across many articles with titles like "10 Amazing Kids Who Are Changing the World!" or "You Won't Believe What These Incredible 20 Teens Are Doing!" In almost every case, there were only one or two girls on each list. This bias appears even more often when you go back in history to look for stories of great girls. This is partly because opportunities for girls were much more limited in the past, but we still need to find and share those stories. *Rad Girls Can* is a start.

MISTY COPELAND

BORN IN KANSAS CITY, MISSOURI, 1982

MISTY COPELAND WAS THIRTEEN years old when she attended her first ballet class on a basketball court at the local Boys and Girls Club. The only reason Misty went was to satisfy her cheerleading coach, who'd observed her remarkable talent and insisted that she give ballet a try. Misty showed up, but for the first few weeks she just watched quietly. Though she loved dancing (she often locked herself in the bathroom to choreograph dance routines to pop songs), she was really shy. Cheerleading had helped her overcome her shyness a little bit, but she was still nervous about trying something new.

After a few weeks of watching, Misty gathered up enough courage to join the class. She had always been an anxious kid who worried about lots of things. She felt embarrassed because all the other girls knew what they were doing, and she felt like she was doing everything wrong. But even though she didn't know the proper positions or the fancy French ballet terms, Misty felt something when she danced. Something . . . *powerful*. She'd never heard classical music before, but she immediately understood the rhythms. She didn't even know what a ballet looked or sounded like, yet she could easily mimic the movements of the much more experienced girls. The teacher, Cindy Bradley, was amazed by Misty's ability to learn quickly and hold challenging positions. She took note of this special new student.

Even though she was new to ballet, Misty had known for some time that she wanted to do something that involved physical movement. At age seven she'd seen a movie about the great gymnast Nadia Comăneci. As Misty watched Nadia flip and fly through the air, she became fascinated with gymnastics. She watched the movie again and again, rewinding the gymnastics scenes. She loved the rhythm and movement of the floor exercises, and began teaching herself cartwheels, handstands, and walkover backbends. That's how Misty realized her natural flexibility—when she tried to do the splits like Nadia, it was easy. She practiced every day, and though she eventually decided that gymnastics wasn't her thing, she'd made an important discovery. After each move she'd throw her arms up like Nadia and pretend that a huge crowd was cheering for her. Misty realized that even though she was shy, she loved the *idea* of performing for a crowd.

Ballet class also offered something that Misty didn't feel at home: a sense of safety and control. Her mom got married and divorced many times, bringing Misty and her five siblings to live in many different homes through the years. Misty never knew how long she and her siblings would stay in one house before they'd have to move. Sometimes they had to leave quickly, with hardly any time to pack their few belongings. There were several years when Misty didn't have a bedroom, or even a bed. Misty never told anyone at school about her chaotic home life. She felt ashamed, and she tried to appear perfect and happy. She spent as much time as possible at her friends' homes and rarely invited anyone to hers.

> "The path to your success is not as fixed and inflexible as you may think."

Soon after Misty began her ballet classes, her mom moved the family once again, to a neighborhood far from the ballet studio. Money was so tight that Misty and her siblings pooled their loose change to buy dinner. Since Misty's mom worked twelve-hour days and didn't have a car, getting to ballet practice meant a two-hour bus ride. Misty began to doubt whether she could keep going with ballet.

Another thing that worried Misty: she didn't *look* like any of the famous ballerinas in the videos she watched. Those dancers were tall, thin, and always white. Misty was curvy, muscular, and African-American. But thanks to Misty's teacher, and Misty's own deep determination and love for dance, she kept going. She worked incredibly hard, dancing and training every day because she *loved* it. She began to realize that the strong, graceful girl she saw in the studio mirror was *her*. And she was really, really good.

Just eight weeks after her first class, Misty began dancing *en pointe*, meaning she danced on the tips of her toes, wearing special ballet shoes. It's a skill that takes most dancers *years* to perfect. Misty eventually moved in with her teacher so she could attend classes, and by the time she was sixteen, she was being sought after by all of the top American ballet companies, and getting closer to her dream of being the first African-American principal dancer at the American Ballet Theatre (ABT). Principals are the most prestigious dancers in a company and ABT is the most prestigious ballet in the country. They get the biggest roles, have their photos and names appear prominently in programs, and earn the most money. But even more important: they earn the most respect.

At the same time, Misty was dealing with big personal challenges as tensions grew between her mother, who wanted her to live back at home, and her dance teacher, who wanted Misty to stay with her and focus on dance. She was soon caught in the middle of a very public,

very emotional legal battle that taught Misty a great deal about how to trust herself and advocate for what she believes is best for her. Though it was a deeply difficult time for Misty, she continued with both her dance training and her schoolwork, graduating with her class and earning a 3.8 GPA.

By that time, Misty was considered one of the ballet world's brightest stars, and she danced many of the top parts. In 1999, at age seventeen, she joined ABT. Her fame grew, but so did her challenges. She struggled with injuries, body image, and a feeling of isolation as the only black dancer in the company. Unlike most top ballerinas, who are very thin, Misty had an athletic, muscular body. Toward the end of her teenage years she gained weight, and her breasts grew significantly. This impacted everything from her self-esteem to her ability to fit into the small, tight costumes. She was told that she needed to lose weight, and she

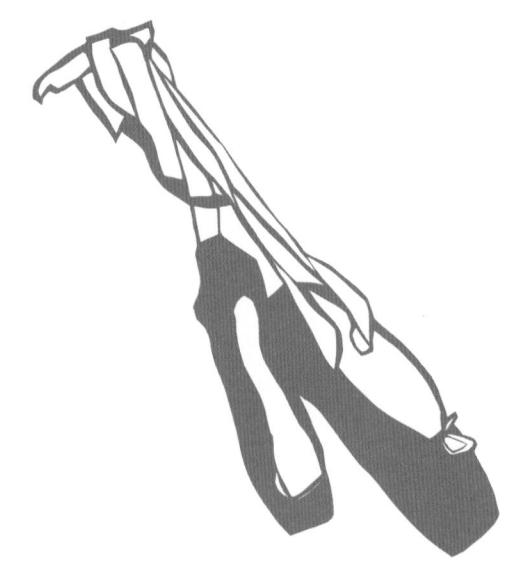

> "I had moments of doubting myself and wanting to quit, because I didn't know that there would be a future for an African-American woman to make it to this level. At the same time, it made me so hungry to push through, to carry the next generation. So it's not me up here—it's everyone that came before me that got me to this position."

felt anxious and self-conscious. For the next several years Misty worked hard to build up her confidence and learn how to love her powerful body and unique shape.

Once again, Misty learned the importance of mentors. She was introduced to older, more experienced black dancers who understood where she was coming from and could offer wisdom and a helping hand. With their support, she learned to see her challenges as assets. Her body—with its injuries, its curves, its color— is exactly what makes her unique. It's what makes her beautiful, athletic, powerful—it's what makes her *Misty*.

Misty continued to dance with passion and integrity, dazzling audiences with her emotional performances. She became a superstar of the dance world, drawing huge crowds to her performances and inspiring a new generation of ballet fans. Finally, in 2015, sixteen years after she joined the ballet company of her dreams, Misty Copeland got her dream position: she was promoted to principal dancer. It was a moment that made headlines, and when she spoke to reporters after the announcement, she acknowledged her challenges, as well as all the dancers who had come before her.

YUSRA MARDINI

BORN IN DAMASCUS, SYRIA, 1998

IT'S JULY OF 2016 at the summer Olympic Games in Rio de Janeiro, Brazil. A young swimmer, Yusra Mardini, crouches on the starting block, waiting for the signal to start the first heat of the 100-meter butterfly race. The spectators are cheering, and somewhere in the crowd are Yusra's parents and sisters, who can't believe they're actually here. The other swimmers crouch and wait, too. Their swim caps display the flags of their nations: Rwanda, Yemen, Qatar, Grenada. But Yusra's cap doesn't have a flag—instead, it displays the five Olympic rings. That's because Yusra no longer has a country, an anthem, or a flag. She is a refugee, and she is swimming as a member of the first-ever Refugee Olympic Team.

The start is signaled, and Yusra dives in, her arms flying through the water in unison, her kick strong and rhythmic. One minute and nine seconds later, she wins her first race as an Olympian. It is a dream come true, but the journey to this moment has been a nightmare. The last time she swam this hard was about two years prior—but she wasn't aiming for a medal then. She wasn't even in a pool. She was in the Mediterranean Sea, aiming for the shores of Greece, and she was trying to save the lives of twenty people.

Yusra grew up in Damascus, the capital of Syria. Her mother was a physical therapist and her father was a swim coach; he began training her when she was three. Her childhood was peaceful and happy. She had lots of friends, enjoyed school, and loved being in the water more than anything. She competed for the Syrian national team and received support from the Syrian Olympic Committee. For a while, the Olympics seemed within her reach, as long as she kept up her training and worked hard.

But in 2011, when she was fourteen, a civil war broke out in Syria. School would sometimes be cancelled for days at a time, and Yusra couldn't train at the pool as often as she liked. Shooting broke out in nearby neighborhoods, and bombs began to fall. Yusra and her family tried to go about their normal lives, but the violence only got worse. In 2012, Yusra's home was destroyed. Two of her fellow swimmers were killed. And a bomb destroyed the roof of the swim center where she trained. Yusra wanted to leave Syria. She wanted to swim again and to lead a normal life. But leaving was not a simple matter. It was impossible for the entire family to leave together, and the journey to safety and freedom was long and dangerous— especially for young women. So they just kept on as best they could.

> "I want to make all the refugees proud of me. It would show that even if we had a tough journey, we can achieve something."

Finally, in 2015, seventeen-year-old Yusra and her older sister, Sara, had the chance to escape. If they could make it to Europe, their parents and little sister could come join them there. To do this, Yusra and Sara would have to make a treacherous and illegal journey across the sea from the shores of Turkey to the shores of Greece. Just getting to Turkey took them one month, and when they finally arrived at the coast, they joined hundreds of other people fleeing dangerous situations. They were led by a team of smugglers into a dense forest, where they hid until it was time to enter the sea. Police helicopters circled overhead, trying to find them. After four days of hiding in the woods, Yusra and Sara were put on a tiny boat with eighteen other people, including a frightened six-year-old boy. The boat was made to hold six people at most.

They set off from the Turkish coast in the evening, but about fifteen minutes into the trip, the motor failed. The boat began to fill with water. And people began to panic. Most of them did not know how to swim, and no one had a life jacket. If they went back to Turkey, they could be arrested and imprisoned. If they did nothing, they would drown. There was no other option: Yusra, her sister, and two others jumped into the cold dark sea, grabbed onto the ropes attached to the boat, and began to swim.

With one hand holding tight to the rope, Yusra relied on her strong legs and one arm. The waters were rough and choppy; her clothing was heavy and the salt water burned her eyes. Eventually the other helpers got too tired and stopped swimming. It was just Yusra and Sara, swimming not just for their own lives but also for the lives of eighteen other Syrians. Sometimes Yusra wanted to stop, but she would look back at the boat and see the terrified little boy. She made funny faces to cheer him up, and she knew she could not give up. She could not stop. She told herself that she was a swimmer—that this was what she was born to do.

They swam for three and a half hours straight until they finally reached the shore, with every refugee still safely onboard the boat. The sisters were exhausted, starving, and barefoot—but they were alive, and they'd made it to Europe. But their journey didn't end there. Yusra and Sara joined thousands of other refugees on foot, on buses, and on trains as they traveled through five different countries. They were often harassed, detained, or denied services by police and citizens who didn't like refugees. But they also encountered kindness: when they arrived in Greece, a young Greek girl saw Yusra's bare feet and offered her her own shoes.

The sisters finally made it to a refugee camp in Germany, and once she was settled, one of the first things Yusra wanted to know was where she could find a pool. An interpreter at the camp connected Yusra to a local swim club, which happened to be one of Berlin's best. Yusra tried out, and though it had been several years since she'd trained, the coaches immediately said yes. She joined the team, and finally, after many years of strife, she was able to train daily.

> "There is no shame in being a refugee if we remember who we are. We are still the doctors, engineers, lawyers, teachers, and students we were back at home. We are still the mothers and fathers, brothers and sisters. It was war and persecution that drove us from our homes in search of peace. That is refugee. That is who I am."

Soon she received the news that she'd been selected to swim in the Olympics as part of the first-ever refugee team. Her nine teammates were also dedicated athletes who'd had to flee their war-torn countries. And they were all honored to represent refugees in the Olympics, to show the world that they are human beings who deserve support and respect. Yusra won her first heat, but she did not win a medal. She won something even more important, though: dignity for herself, and for refugees worldwide.

In 2016, Yusra became a Goodwill Ambassador for the United Nations Refugee Agency. She has shared her story and spoken on behalf of refugees in front of world leaders; she has met with the pope and President Barack Obama. And Yusra is not done competing. She may not know which country she'll represent, but she plans to compete in future Olympic Games.

CLARESSA SHIELDS

Claressa Shields started boxing when she was eleven years old. At fifteen, she declared that she was going to be the greatest female boxer of all time. And at seventeen she went to London and became the first American woman to win an Olympic gold medal in boxing. Claressa is definitely one of the best—but her path to greatness has not been easy.

> "If you're having a bad day and it seems like it's never going to get better, think of me. I dreamed about reaching a goal and I made it happen. You can, too. I'm living proof of that."

Even before she put on gloves and stepped into the ring, Claressa was a fighter. She grew up in a troubled neighborhood. Her father was in prison, and her mom was an alcoholic. Claressa and her siblings were often left alone without food, and Claressa slept on the floor most nights. When her mom was home, she often had friends over. Several of these men abused Claressa, but she was too afraid to tell anyone. These experiences filled her with shame and anger.

When she was nine, Claressa's father got out of jail. He'd once been a boxer, and he wanted someone to continue his legacy. "What about me?" Claressa asked.

He laughed and told her, "It's a man's sport. You're too pretty to box."

Claressa was furious. "I don't want to be a model," she replied. "I want to be an athlete. A boxer. Like *you*." She went to a local gym and told the boxing coach she wanted to learn. Right away, he was impressed—but Claressa had to get permission from her dad to join the gym and sign up for lessons.

A few days later she went to her dad's house and was surprised to see her stepmom and several siblings there. They were smiling, and her dad handed her the signed permission slip. "We took a family vote," he explained. "You won." He paid sixty dollars to sign her up for lessons, and from that day on, Claressa trained almost every day. She learned speed, power, strategy, and technique. Boxing helped her manage her emotions and channel her anger into her powerful punches.

By age sixteen, her record was nineteen wins and zero losses, and she won a spot on the first-ever Olympic women's boxing team. No one thought she'd win, but she proved them all wrong. When she stood on the podium and heard the announcer say, "Claressa Shields, gold medal winner," she couldn't believe her ears. Four years later, she won her second gold, becoming the first American boxer (male or female) to win *two* gold medals.

MARY BETH TINKER

BORN IN DES MOINES, IOWA, 1952

THE YEAR WAS 1965. The Vietnam War was escalating, and so were the protests against it. College students and peace activists organized marches, sit-ins, rallies, and loud demonstrations on college campuses and in cities across the country. The United States had no clear objectives in the conflict, yet 180,000 American troops were fighting in a war that many saw as pointless. For the first time in American history, everyday citizens could see footage of war on their television sets. Every evening the nightly news shows broadcast frightening images of bombed villages, innocent children injured and killed, and the caskets of American soldiers.

One of the many Americans who saw these chilling images was eighth grader Mary Beth Tinker, who watched the news each night with her family. The Tinkers were horrified by what they saw. Mary Beth didn't understand all of the complex politics of the war, but she knew she was opposed to it.

Mary Beth was raised with a strong sense of social justice. Her father was a Methodist minister, and her family later became involved with the Quakers. The Tinkers believed in putting their faith into action, and joined the civil rights movement to picket for fair housing and employment where they lived. Her older sister attended the March on Washington for racial equality in 1963. And during the summer of 1964, when Mary Beth was eleven, her parents went to Mississippi to take a stand against the Ku Klux Klan's racist violence, and to help register black people to vote as part of the Freedom Summer campaign. Mary Beth was inspired by such bravery, and by the stories of many courageous young people who were

involved in the civil rights movement. When it came time for Mary Beth to make her own statement, she had plenty of strong examples to draw from.

Mary Beth, her brother, and a number of other students came up with a simple, peaceful plan to show their opposition to the war. They would wear black armbands to school. The armbands would show support for a Christmas truce, and serve as a sign of mourning for the people who'd died on *both* sides of the war. Mary Beth and the others were sad about the loss of American lives, but they also mourned the lives of the Vietnamese who were killed. This made their plan especially controversial when it was discovered by the school principal. It was considered "un-American" for these young people to show concern for the lives of the Vietnamese people affected by the war.

> "In a democracy, the people who are affected by decisions are supposed to be the ones who have the right to speak on their own behalf, and this should include young people."

The principal found out about the armband plan because a student wrote an article about it for the school newspaper. Two days before they planned to wear them, the principal and the school board held an emergency meeting. They passed a new rule banning armbands. Most of the kids who'd planned to wear them backed out, not wanting to get in trouble.

Mary Beth was faced with a dilemma. She had always believed in following the rules. As an eighth grader, Mary Beth was one of the youngest of the group planning the protest— most of the others were in high school, and some were in college. She was respectful of her parents and teachers, and she didn't like to cause trouble. But she felt that the principal and school board were wrong. She was deeply opposed to the war and felt that she had a right to express that.

Mary Beth's parents had grown up during World War II, and they had often told their children about the many German citizens who knew what was going on but did not speak up in the early days of the Holocaust. Her parents had taught her that you have to speak your conscience. So Mary Beth broke the rule. On December 17, 1965, she came to school wearing a black armband.

She was promptly suspended and sent home, as were her brother John and three others. Mary Beth's younger sister Hope and brother Paul also decided to wear armbands, but they were not suspended. The news of these young students who just wanted to wear armbands spread beyond Iowa and soon made national headlines. Mary Beth and her family received supportive messages about their commitment to free speech, but they were also harassed. Red paint was thrown at their house, and they received angry phone calls. One day Mary Beth answered the phone and a woman said, "Is this Mary Beth Tinker?" Mary Beth said yes, and the woman threatened to kill her. Mary Beth hung up the phone, terrified. A death threat because of an armband? Because she believed in peace?

The following week Mary Beth and her parents attended a school board meeting to appeal the decision. Two hundred people showed up: some were there to praise the board for stopping the protest, but many others were there to support the students. People argued for more than two hours, but the board wouldn't change its mind. The armbands remained prohibited. But the Tinker family was not about to give up. They went to the American Civil Liberties Union

(ACLU), which was willing to take on their case and argue that suspending the students for wearing armbands was a violation of their First Amendment rights. In other words, their freedom of speech had been violated.

Mary Beth didn't feel hopeful about the court case. It was hard for her to imagine that a big important judge was going to allow kids to break the rules. And the first judge did dismiss their case, but that wasn't the end of it. Three years after she wore the armband, the Tinker case ended up going all the way to the U.S. Supreme Court, thanks to the commitment of several passionate lawyers and the courage of Mary Beth, her brother John, and another student plaintiff named Chris Eckhardt. With support from the ACLU, the students and their families refused to drop the case.

On February 24, 1969, the court ruled seven to two in favor of Mary Beth Tinker and the students. The court said that the district had violated Mary Beth's First Amendment rights, and the majority wrote that students and teachers do not "shed their constitutional rights to freedom of speech or expression at the schoolhouse gate." This landmark decision, known as *Tinker vs. Des Moines*, established the free speech rights of all students in public schools, and said that students cannot be censored unless they are disrupting the educational process. It is one of the most important legal cases affecting young people and their rights to free expression in schools. And it's all because a group of young people—including a thirteen-year-old girl—had the courage to do what was right.

THE CLIMATE KIDS

There are many ways that young people can help protect and preserve the environment. You can recycle, compost, and conserve water and electricity. Another option? You can sue the federal government—as Hazel Van Ummersen, Victoria Barrett, Jaime Butler, and Jayden Fontlin did. They're among twenty-one climate activists under age twenty-one who are plaintiffs in a landmark court case.

> "It's important that I'm doing this at a young age because it inspires people of my generation to help. You don't have to wait until you're older."
> —Jayden Fontlin

A plaintiff is an individual who brings a case to court (as opposed to the defendant, whom the case is brought against). In this case, the defendant is the president of the United States, and the plaintiff is a group of young people who argue that the U.S. government has actively contributed to climate change. By doing so, the government is violating the constitutional rights of young people. The plaintiffs argue that having a healthy climate is a fundamental liberty for today's children and the children of the future.

The plaintiffs range in age from eleven to twenty-one and come from all over the United States. They've all witnessed the impact of climate change on their lives in many different ways. Some come from urban areas—like eighteen-year-old Victoria, whose school shut down after Superstorm Sandy flooded New York City. Seventeen-year-old Jaime lives with her family on a Navajo reservation in Arizona, where a devastating drought has dried up the natural springs that her family has relied on for generations. Fourteen-year-old Jayden, who is from Louisiana, has already experienced two floods in her home caused in part by rising sea levels along the Gulf Coast.

The plaintiffs don't argue the case in front of the judges—they have grown-up lawyers who do that. Their job is to tell their personal stories of how climate change impacts them. They attend as many of the court hearings as possible, and they also act as spokespeople for this important lawsuit. In the process, they get to learn a great deal about law, government, the judicial process, the science behind climate change, and what it means to be a climate activist.

Thirteen-year-old Hazel joined the lawsuit because she is concerned about climate change and wants to show that young people "aren't just playing video games on the couch." Her friends think it's cool that she's part of this big lawsuit, and, she says, no matter what happens with the suit—whether they win or lose—she knows she'll be fighting to protect our planet for the rest of her life.

MADISON KIMREY

BORN IN BURLINGTON, NORTH CAROLINA, 2001

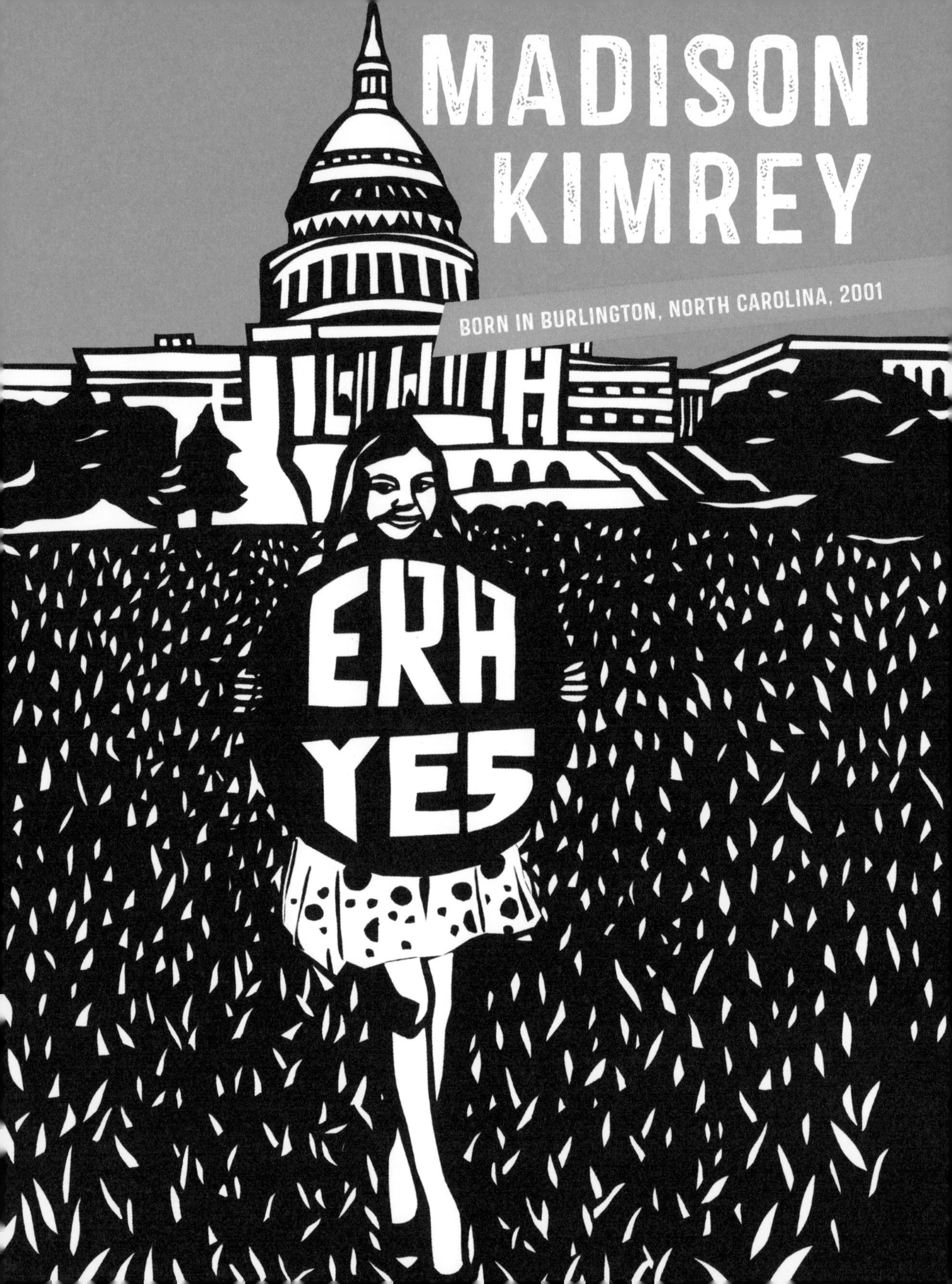

DURING THE SUMMER OF 2013, Madison Kimrey was using Twitter to watch a live debate between two of her state senators. This might seem like a weird thing for a twelve-year-old to be doing on a lovely summer day, but Madison is *really* into politics, and the senators were debating something that directly impacts young people: the elimination of voter preregistration.

> "I have two choices: I can be what other people want me to be, or I can live my truth and be the change I want to see in the world."

In the United States, you have to be eighteen to vote, but many states allow younger people to preregister so that when they turn eighteen they're automatically ready to cast their first vote. In Madison's state of North Carolina in 2013, sixteen- and seventeen-year-olds could preregister when they got a driver's license or through voting awareness programs in high schools. In the year 2012 alone, fifty thousand teens preregistered. Madison was already looking forward to preregistering herself.

But the new governor of North Carolina, Pat McCrory, had changed the rules as part of a series of changes to voting laws that made it harder for *many* North Carolinians to vote. Even though Madison wasn't old enough to vote—or even to preregister—she felt passionate about the issue, and she wanted to know *why* the leader of her state would make it harder for young people to register.

Her first step was to start a blog to express her thoughts on politics. She quickly gained followers, many of whom were surprised to

learn that the eloquent, thoughtful posts were written by a seventh grader. Then she began reading about voting rights and state politics, and she learned about Moral Mondays, a nonviolent protest movement. Every Monday, a diverse group of people who were upset with Governor McCrory would gather at the state capital to make their voices heard by giving speeches and holding sit-ins.

Madison convinced her parents to give her a ride to the next Moral Mondays event. She met and talked with activists from many groups, but she learned the most by just listening. She returned every Monday, often perching up in a tree so she could see and hear as much as possible. There, this young activist could study her elders closely. It was almost like a classroom. She observed how people spoke with passion and respect; she saw how they remained calm yet committed, and how they spoke and fought for the rights of *everyone*. Though she was decades younger than most of the attendees, she felt respected.

> "It's time for people to wake up and realize that, like it or not, kids like me are going to run the country someday."

Witnessing these conversations gave Madison an idea: she should have a conversation with the governor and ask him why he wanted to restrict the voting rights of so many North Carolinians. She started a petition that included a letter to Governor McCrory: "I would like to discuss the part of HB589 that deals with the ability of sixteen- and seventeen-year-olds to preregister to vote. I don't wish to debate you; I just want you to hear what I have to say and I want to hear what you have to say." Her goal was to get a hundred signatures. She got more than twelve thousand—and she delivered them in person to the governor's office. That got his attention, but she didn't get the meeting. Instead, Governor McCrory went on a local radio program and called Madison a "prop," saying that her request was "ridiculous."

> "I feel it's part of my civic responsibility to use my voice to help build the kind of future I want, not just for myself but for my country."

Ridiculous? A prop? When Madison heard this, she was *not* happy. So she did what she'd become used to doing: she got up and gave a speech about it. At a meeting attended by hundreds of community members, she declared, "I am *not* a prop! I am part of the new generation of suffragettes. And I will not stand silent while laws are passed to reduce the amount of voter turnout by young people in my home state."

The video of Madison's speech went viral. People all over the country were impressed by this bold young woman and her simple yet powerful request. They were less impressed with the governor, who had dismissed this intelligent young person. Her story appeared in many publications, and she was even interviewed on TV by the famous civil rights activist Al Sharpton. When Mr. Sharpton asked Madison why she was getting involved in the voting rights issue, she answered, "I didn't like what I saw happening to my state, so I wanted to take action and see what I could do to stop it." For Madison, it's as simple as that. Don't like what's happening? Get involved. Do something.

And she did. Madison spent the next three years writing articles and blog posts, giving speeches, and talking to anyone she could about voting rights. She studied the words

and actions of female leaders like Wendy Davis, Gloria Steinem, and Hillary Clinton. She was persistent and stubborn—and it paid off. The pressure to change the laws never let up, and in 2016, a court overturned Governor McCrory's voter laws, ruling that they were unconstitutional. Preregistration was reinstated, meaning that Madison—and every sixteen- and seventeen-year-old—will get to preregister from now on. In November 2020, you'll find Madison at the voting booth, casting her first ballot. And in November 2040? Well, we might just be voting for President Kimrey!

MARY-PAT HECTOR

Mary-Pat Hector's campaign for an open seat on the city council of Stonecrest, Georgia, hadn't even gotten started before someone tried to stop it. Not because of her political beliefs or some past scandal, but because of her age. An award-winning nineteen-year-old college sophomore, Mary-Pat had years of experience as an activist, youth leader, and public speaker, and was eager to launch her political career. But one of her opponents objected and wrote a letter to the County Board of Elections, arguing that she was just too young to run.

> **"The fact that young people all over the country saw me running, and knew they could run, too—that was the most meaningful part of it."**

Mary-Pat thought this was ridiculous: at age nineteen she had the right to vote, but she couldn't be elected to represent her community? She appeared before the board and argued that she should be allowed to run. Her friends and family packed the courtroom, and the board ruled unanimously in her favor. Mary-Pat could remain on the ballot.

Mary-Pat and her team (who were all college students) worked hard on her campaign. They knocked on doors, handed out flyers, and made phone calls to voters. Mary-Pat still faced doubt from people who couldn't imagine someone as young as her being their representative. Some told her to "wait her turn" and questioned how she would balance political responsibilities with schoolwork. But others were excited by her energy and vision, and she received mail from young people all over the country who were inspired by her campaign.

Mary-Pat didn't win the race, but she lost by only twenty-two votes. And she may have scored an even greater victory: her story inspired a Georgia state senator to write a bill making it a state law that anyone eighteen and older can run for office. And, Mary-Pat says, her campaign was just the first of many to come.

ASHIMA SHIRAISHI

BORN IN NEW YORK, NEW YORK, 2001

Ashima Shiraishi is considered by many to be one of the best rock climbers alive. Not the best *girl* climber or the best *young* climber, but one of the best climbers, period.

It all began in New York City's Central Park, where a large, wide rock in the middle of the park caught six-year-old Ashima's eye. It's known as Rat Rock, and it's popular with climbers who scale its craggy sides. Little Ashima watched in awe as people (mostly grown-ups) climbed like spiders to reach the top. Then she tried it herself—and that was that. She began climbing Rat Rock every day after school, and soon her dad began taking her to an indoor climbing gym. She won her first climbing competition at age seven.

> "I climb for myself."

Bouldering routes (known as "problems") are ranked on a scale of 0 to 15, with V15 being the absolute most difficult problem. At age eight, Ashima became the youngest person in the world to complete (or "send") a V10. Two years later, she sent a V13, and a few days before her fifteenth birthday, Ashima successfully completed a climb called Horizon on Mount Hiei in Japan, making her the first woman and the youngest person *ever* to send a V15 boulder problem.

Climbing requires many skills. Yes, you have to be physically strong and flexible, but the sport is also very mental. Focus, patience, and strategic thinking are crucial. "Climbing is like solving a puzzle," Ashima explains. "You have to think about how you're going to move to each hold." Climbers like Ashima can spend days, weeks, or even *months* studying, planning, and then trying to conquer each climb, which usually involves a *lot* of falling. Ashima failed at Horizon three times before getting it. "Sometimes it seems impossible," she says, "but I always have to remind myself that anything is possible."

When she was fourteen, Ashima fell forty-five feet at an indoor climbing gym and was rushed to the hospital. Luckily, she had sustained only bruises and a sore back. The serious fall didn't make her want to quit—in fact, it had the opposite effect. She won a major national competition several days later. "I feel like that injury made me think about how valuable climbing is to my life," she said. "I think it made me grow as a climber."

SKY BROWN

BORN IN MIYAZAKI, JAPAN, 2008

In the summer of 2016, a skater named Sky Brown competed in the Vans U.S. Open, a major skateboarding competition. In front of a huge cheering crowd and live television cameras, Sky dropped into the bowl and immediately nailed a frontside noseblunt, an incredibly hard and dangerous trick. The crowd went wild, and the announcers were amazed. "Half of the pro guys competing here can't do that trick!" exclaimed one announcer. The reason he was so impressed? Sky had just turned eight years old—and Sky is a girl. In fact, she was the youngest girl to ever compete in that competition. But after she landed the sweet move, she fell off her board. What did she do? She got right back on it and continued to blow everyone away.

Sky's mom and dad are both surfers and skaters, and they've always encouraged her to go for it. When she was really little, her dad would bring her along to the skate park and the beach. As she watched the adults and big kids, she realized that she wanted to try it too. She started skateboarding at age three and learned to surf at four. And she hasn't stopped since.

> **"When there's a bunch of boys skating, you don't have to be afraid. You just gotta *go*."**

Sky is already great at what she does, but she's always trying to get better and learn new tricks. To do this, she practices almost every day, watches her favorite skaters and surfers on YouTube, and takes big risks. She knows that you have to fail lots of times before you finally perfect a new move. Sometimes that means falling in front of friends or wiping out on a big wave, which can be embarrassing—and painful. Scrapes and bruises are a reality, and there's always the potential for more serious injury. But for Sky, the feeling she gets when she's going super high on her board on a ramp or riding on top of a big swell makes it all worth it. And safety is important: she always wears a helmet and full pads (elbow, knee, and wrist) when skateboarding, and she never goes out alone. Skating and surfing with friends keeps her safe—and it's also what makes it so fun!

THE SCHIMMEL SISTERS

BORN ON THE UMATILLA INDIAN RESERVATION, OREGON, 1992 (SHONI) AND 1993 (JUDE)

Jude and Shoni Schimmel are sisters, championship basketball players, and beloved role models to tens of thousands of Native American fans who follow their every move.

Jude and Shoni grew up on the Umatilla Indian Reservation in eastern Oregon along with their six siblings. Life on a reservation (often referred to as "rez") has many advantages, but it also comes with challenges, especially for young people. Opportunities to succeed can be limited, and teen suicide rates on reservations are three to ten times higher than the national average. Women like the Schimmel sisters represent hope for many young Native Americans, who see them as proof that Indians can achieve great things "off the rez."

The sisters each started playing basketball around age four, and when Shoni was seven, she announced that she wanted to play in the Women's National Basketball Association (WNBA) someday. The girls played and practiced constantly, competing in (and dominating) local tournaments. Their style of playing is known as "rez ball," a uniquely fast-paced, creative style of basketball played on Native American reservations across the country. When Shoni was a junior in high school, her mom was offered a job coaching basketball in a town off the reservation. Shoni played while her mom coached, and they led the team to the state semifinals. By her senior year, Shoni was one of the nation's top players. She chose to play for top-ranked Division I Louisville, and Jude soon joined her there. Shoni was a four-year starter and led the team to a championship.

In 2014, Shoni became a WNBA first-round draft pick out of Louisville, and in her first WNBA season she became the league's first rookie All-Star Game MVP. During her senior year, Jude helped lead Louisville to yet another incredible season, and she was soon drafted to play ball overseas in Spain.

> **"We want to be that light of hope for younger generations. We want them to know it is possible. If you put your mind and heart into it, you can achieve anything you want."**
> **—Jude Schimmel**

The sisters' fans travel all over to attend games and cheer for them, often holding up signs that say things like "Rez Girls Rock," "Native Pride," and "Never Give Up." Often fans write on their signs both the name of their tribe and the many hundreds (or even thousands) of miles they traveled to see the Schimmels play. They mob the sisters for autographs, and they often tell them, tearfully, how much it means to them to see young Native American women do so well.

Jude and Shoni know that more is riding on them than just winning games. Their enormous fan base is depending on them to succeed, and they're proud to work hard and represent their community.

MUSLIM GIRLS MAKING CHANGE

FOUNDED IN BURLINGTON, VERMONT, 2015

WHEN TENTH GRADER Hawa Adam saw the flyer in the school hallway for a slam poetry team competition, she knew just what to do. "Okay, guys," Hawa told her friends Kiran, Lena, and Balkisa, "we have to prepare something. We have to do this." Did it matter that two of the four girls had never written a poem? And that the other two had only recently discovered slam poetry as a powerful form of expression? No. For four brown-skinned Muslim girls growing up in Vermont, what mattered were the stories they wanted to tell and the emotions they wanted to convey.

Slam poetry is a creative competition. Poets don't just recite their poems; they perform them and vie for the highest score (though any slam poet will tell you, "It's not about the points, it's about the poetry"). The poems are often political and personal, and the style of performance tends to be intense and powerful.

The four friends called their team Muslim Girls Making Change (MGMC), and they worked together for weeks to write their first poem. "Wake Up America" is about the tragic events of September 11, 2001, and how American Muslims became the targets of suspicion, harassment, and even violence in the months and years that followed.

> "We write poems about things that we can't keep inside of us anymore."

MGMC went to the audition and blew away the judges, who immediately signed them up to represent the state of Vermont at the international Brave New Voices slam poetry competition. Just a few months after the audition, the girls took a twenty-hour car ride to Washington, DC, where they became the first all-Muslim team to perform. They didn't win, but they were a huge hit.

Hawa, Kiran, Lena, and Balkisa had met at their local Islamic Community Center, where they bonded over many things, including their shared experiences as Muslim girls in Vermont. Vermont is the second whitest state in America, and while people of any race or ethnicity can be Muslim, the members of MGMC are all brown-skinned. As a result, the girls are constantly asked questions about their identities. They know that many of the questions aren't intended to be offensive, but they get tired of having to explain their own existence.

Their poem "Hijab 101" is a humorous—but also serious—attempt to answer the endless inquiries the girls receive about their *hijabs*, the traditional Muslim head coverings they all wear every day. The poem is especially powerful for Kiran, who didn't begin wearing her hijab until she was in tenth grade. She *wanted* to wear it, but in middle school she just wanted to fit in. She was afraid of looking different and of being judged. She felt proud once she began to wear her hijab to school, and she used her experiences to help craft the poem, which begins with a list of frequently asked questions: "Aren't you hot in that/Do you shower with that on?/What's underneath that thing?/Why do you wear that?/You were prettier before./Can I see your hair?/Does your dad make you wear it?"

MGMC have performed their poems all over their home state and beyond, and they've expanded their subject matter as well. They address many contemporary issues and injustices, from police brutality to the ways that immigrants are viewed in America. They also lead poetry and performance workshops, where they show other young people how to use poetry to express emotions and experiences that the world needs to hear.

TAVI GEVINSON

WHEN ELEVEN-YEAR-OLD Tavi Gevinson started her fashion blog, *Style Rookie,* she had no idea what it would lead to. She didn't *mean* to become one of the most well-known bloggers in the fashion world. She had no idea she'd end up sitting front-row at New York Fashion Week, hugging and cheek-kissing her fashion designer idols. And she definitely didn't think that four years after starting her blog, she'd be the editor in chief of the most popular online teen publication in the country. But that's what happened.

Tavi grew up with a love of performance and theater, which included a fondness for dress-up and costumes. She was interested in fashion and art from an early age and began experimenting with her outfits in sixth grade, wearing bright patterns, vintage clothes, funky shoes, and wild accessories. In middle school it felt like everyone was trying to fit in, wearing the same clothes from the same stores in the same malls. Tavi felt rejected by most of the cliques at school, and she decided that if she wasn't going to fit in, she'd just embrace that.

> **"If you are intimidated by the artists who came before you, understand you too have a place, right next to them."**

By creating a look all her own, Tavi felt free from the daily anxiety of having to look like everyone else. She mixed thrift-store clothes with oversized shirts borrowed from her siblings. She wore bright floral patterns and stripes and fringed vests and platform sandals. She dyed her blonde hair gray and often topped off her looks with random headpieces like flower crowns, lace doilies, or enormous cartoonish hair bows.

It worked for Tavi, but it did *not* go over too well with her peers. Especially the boys, who teased her relentlessly. Sometimes they even seemed mad at Tavi for her outfits, like they were offended that she wasn't trying to impress them. Her reaction was to write down all the insults in her journals and then to wear something even weirder the next day. If a boy sneered at her and told her she looked like a freak, she'd show up the next morning wearing a tutu, silently daring him to tease her again.

> **"Fashion can be about having fun and expressing yourself—it doesn't have to be about being pretty."**

When Tavi learned about fashion blogs from a friend's older sister, she decided to start one of her own. It seemed like a fun way for her to document her outfits, her classmates' responses to those outfits, and her various pop-culture obsessions. She set up a simple blog and got started. Her first post was titled "The New Girl in Town"; it began, "Lately I've been really interested in fashion." She posted regularly on her blog and on the blogs of fellow fashion-obsessed people. Tavi's quirky fashion sense combined with her unique writing style soon attracted lots of followers.

By the time Tavi was in seventh grade, *Style Rookie* had more than thirty thousand daily readers—and adults in the fashion world were paying attention to this girl in the Chicago suburbs. She even received invitations to attend New York Fashion Week, as well as fashion shows in Paris. While many in the fashion world adored her blog and loved meeting her, others were suspicious. It was hard for some adults to believe that Tavi really was . . . well, *real*. Was her blog actually written by an adult pretending to be a teenager? Were her parents the ones writing it? Can a seventh grader really talk about homework *and* the new Prada collection in the same sentence? Did she *belong* at Fashion Week? Can a twelve-year-old be *this cool*?

The sudden attention (both positive and negative) overwhelmed Tavi at first. Her confidence was growing, though, and she believed that her bold self-expression was having a positive impact on her readers as well as her classmates (who were beginning to appreciate her outfits). In addition to loving fashion, she loved writing about it, and she began to imagine a future as a writer. With the help of her family, Tavi worked to balance her newfound fame with her regular life, and to ignore the critics. Still, it was surreal for her to go to New York City for a weekend of parties and runway shows and then be back in math class on Monday morning, taking a test. In one post on *Style Rookie,* she reflected on how she felt while sitting next to Anna Wintour, the very famous editor of *Vogue* magazine: "I felt like I was watching everything going on around me through a window. Usually I could see out of it, but every once in a while, I was forced to look at my own reflection, which was less fun."

Tavi continued *Style Rookie* through eighth grade, and she kept attending fashion shows and interviewing famous designers. But by the time she was in high school, she was ready to explore new topics, especially around feminism and the complexities of teen-girl identity.

She read magazines and websites aimed at teen girls, but she didn't feel like any of them got it quite right. It felt like the world expected girls to fit neatly into one box or another: Either you could be popular *or* you could be alternative. You could play sports *or* be good

at math and science. You could be a feminist *or* be into fashion and makeup. If you fit into multiple boxes or weren't sure where you wanted to be, or if you just rejected the idea of boxes and labels and cliques altogether— well, people got confused. Tavi also knew how much pressure there was on girls to feel cool, and she wanted girls to know that they were *already* cool enough and smart enough and pretty enough. Nobody is perfect, and even the most confident feminist heroes feel insecure and have bad days.

> "Feminism is not a rulebook but a discussion, a conversation, a process."

She announced the idea for a new publication dedicated to these topics (and called simply *Rookie*), and she asked her readers to submit their ideas. She received three thousand emails right away and knew she was on to something. *Rookie* became one of the most successful online publications for girls, with Tavi serving as owner and editor in chief. *Rookie* publishes writing, photography, and other forms of artwork by and for teenagers (they also publish work by grown-ups, *and* sometimes grown-ups read Rookie, too.)

By the time she turned twenty, Tavi was managing a staff of more than eighty people. She has edited four books, interviewed countless creative people, and even returned to her theater roots, appearing on Broadway and in several films. She speaks regularly about art, feminism, girlhood, nostalgia, politics, and whatever else she's fascinated with.

EGYPT "IFY" UFELE

Every year the fashion world turns its eyes to New York and its legendary Fashion Week. This is when all the big designers debut their new collections. Models walk the runways, and celebrities clamor to sit in the front rows. It's a big fancy deal, and in 2016, Egypt Ufele—who goes by her nickname, Ify—became one of many talented designers to debut her fashion line there.

Her designs are bright and bold, with prints inspired by her parents' native country of Nigeria. But a few things about Ify's collection, Chubiiline, really made her stand out from the crowd: her clothes are made for women with bodies that are bigger and curvier than the average fashion model's. And at the time of her debut, Ify was ten years old, making her the youngest designer ever to show at Fashion Week.

> **"I turned negative attention into positive attention."**

It all began because of bullies. Ify had a severe asthmatic condition that required her to take medication that affected her weight and her ability to exercise. Aside from her asthma, she was healthy; she just had a bigger body than most of her peers. Unfortunately, this was a problem for some kids. They called her names and laughed at her because of her weight, and a few times they were even physically harmful to her. Rather than just feel sad about it, Ify wanted to do something.

One of Ify's favorite hobbies is sewing. She learned to use a sewing machine from her grandmother, Nellie, and she'd spend hours making clothes for her dolls. One day it occurred to her that she could make more than just doll clothes— what if she made her *own* clothes? Because of her body shape, Ify had a hard time finding cute clothes that fit her right. She thought about what she'd like to wear, did some sketches, and voilà! Ify started making clothes for herself, her family, and plus-size people.

Her designs quickly got attention. With the help of her mom, Reba, Ify started her own clothing company, and soon her dresses, gowns, tops, and skirts were cruising down the runway. Her designs are now in boutiques and stores across New York, and Ify also visits schools to talk to other young people about how to deal with bullying. As for the kids who bullied her? They've all apologized, Ify says.

ANNE FRANK

ON THE MORNING OF her thirteenth birthday, Anne Frank received many gifts—a bouquet of roses and some peonies, a blue blouse, a puzzle, a gift certificate for two books, and a strawberry tart from her mother. But the most beloved present was a small notebook with a red-and-white-checked cover. Anne was delighted to begin a diary, recording her life, thoughts, and ideas in the little notebook. When Anne's family was forced to go into hiding during World War II, she brought the diary with her, and for the next two years she would fill it (plus several additional notebooks), documenting her fears, her frustrations, her dreams and desires.

In the end, Anne did not survive—but her diary did. It was published by her father in 1947 and has been translated into sixty-seven languages, with more than thirty million copies sold worldwide. Anne's story is widely known around the world—for many people, she is their introduction to the Holocaust. She has become one of the twentieth century's most famous girls, but even though her story is well known, it's worth revisiting again and again. Anne Frank has much to teach us about our history, our present, and our future.

> "I want to write, but more than that, I want to bring out all kinds of things that lie buried deep in my heart."

Anne was born in Frankfurt, Germany, on June 12, 1929. When Anne was four, Adolf Hitler and the Nazis took control of Germany and began to arrest, attack, and even kill people who were Jewish (they also targeted Gypsies, people with physical or mental disabilities, homosexuals, people with dark skin, and others). Anne, her parents, and her seven-year-old sister, Margot, fled to the city of Amsterdam, where they thought they'd be safe. Anne's father, Otto, started a business, and Anne had a happy childhood. She learned to speak Dutch and was a cheerful girl with many friends.

> "Writing in a diary is a really strange experience for someone like me. Not only because I've never written anything before, but also because it seems to me that later on neither I nor anyone else will be interested in the musings of a thirteen-year-old schoolgirl."

But in 1940 the Germans invaded the Netherlands and took control of the country. Amsterdam was no longer safe. Jews had to wear yellow stars on their clothing and were not allowed to own bicycles or radios.

In Germany and other Nazi-occupied countries, Jews were being sent to so-called concentration camps. Otto feared this would soon happen in Holland, and for months he tried to bring his family to America. He wrote many letters to his contacts in the United States, including a friend from college who worked for the government and was the son of a prominent businessman. Though this friend did try to help him, the Frank family was denied visas, due to tightened immigration restrictions and anti-immigrant feelings in America. In 1942 Otto's fears came true: young Margot was called up to a German "work camp." The next day, the Franks went into hiding in a cramped two-room "annex" hidden behind Otto's office. His loyal employees agreed to protect them. The Franks were soon joined by four others.

> "After the war I'd like to publish a book called *The Secret Annex*. It remains to be seen whether I'll succeed."

Anne wrote in her diary constantly. Writing was a way to quietly pass the time (the family often had to be silent in the annex so they wouldn't be discovered). But writing was also Anne's passion—she dreamed of becoming a published writer, and her imagination was filled with stories. In her diary she writes about her school friends, as well as the war. She gives detailed descriptions of the annex and captures the terror and anxiety of war. She writes about her crush on Peter, the teenage boy who also lives in the annex, and she expresses her frustrations with her mother and the other adults. Even under frightening, oppressive

conditions, Anne experiences emotions and feelings familiar to almost all young people—she wants love, affection, attention. She experiences joy and desire, but she also feels self-conscious and nervous.

Anne Frank didn't keep just *one* diary—in fact, she filled the pages of the original red-and-white-checked book in less than a year. She used other notebooks to record more than thirty short stories, and even used a cashbook (what a banker like her father would use) to copy all the "beautiful sentences" that she came across in the books she read. The amount of writing that Anne was able to produce in two years is a testament to her talent.

On March 28, 1944, Anne heard a radio broadcast that called on the Dutch people to keep diaries, letters, and other documents to help maintain recollections of wartime life once the occupation was over. Anne realized that she could be published and achieve her dreams

of becoming a writer. She continued the diary entries, detailing her day-to-day feelings and emotions, but she also started a new project: a novel called *Het Auchterhuis* (which translates roughly to *"The Annex"*), which combined past diary entries with new ideas. Anne wrote with a reader in mind—she used pseudonyms (fake names) and carefully edited and crafted the story. In seventy-six days she filled two hundred pieces of paper—but she never finished it.

> "I can shake off everything as I write; my sorrows disappear; my courage is reborn. But, and that's a big question, will I ever be able to write something great, will I ever become a journalist or a writer?"

On August 4, 1944, Nazi soldiers discovered the annex. Anne and the seven others were arrested and transported to the concentration camp at Auschwitz. After seven brutal months, Anne died of typhus, a contagious disease. She was fifteen years old. The only member of the Frank family to survive was Otto, who was able to return to Amsterdam and reunite with his former employees. His trusted friend Miep Gies had found Anne's diaries and a bundle of loose notes after the raid. She had saved them, hoping to return them to Anne. Instead, she gave them to Otto, who'd had no idea that his daughter was such a committed and gifted writer. He wanted to keep it all private, but he was so moved by Anne's desire to be a published author that he decided to share her words with the world.

> "I want to be useful or bring enjoyment to all people, even those I've never met. I want to go on living even after my death!"

Diaries are often seen as personal and private, and the diaries of young girls in particular are not usually taken seriously. But as Anne Frank shows us, diaries can have great power. They can contain *anything*, from the writer's deepest thoughts and feelings to creative stories, poems, and plays. A diary might hold detailed accounts of everyday life, as well as insight into major political or cultural events. They help us remember who we were and how we lived. Eleanor Roosevelt called Anne's work "one of the wisest and most moving commentaries on war and its impact on human beings that I have ever read." Anne Frank's diaries give us insight into the devastating effects of war—and into the complex mind and heart of an extraordinary girl.

> "It's a wonder I haven't abandoned all my ideals, they seem so absurd and impractical. Yet I cling to them because I still believe, in spite of everything, that people are truly good at heart. It's utterly impossible for me to build my life on a foundation of chaos, suffering, and death. I see the world being slowly transformed into a wilderness, I hear the approaching thunder that, one day, will destroy us too, I feel the suffering of millions. And yet, when I look up at the sky, I somehow feel that everything will change for the better, that this cruelty too shall end, that peace and tranquility will return once more."

MALALA YOUSAFZAI

Malala Yousafzai's incredible journey through violence and survival to worldwide acclaim began with a series of online diary entries that were published by the British Broadcasting Company (BBC). A journalist wanted to find a young person to offer his or her version of life under Taliban rule in Pakistan. The Taliban, an extremist group, had ordered many schools closed, and eleven-year-old Malala was eager to share her experiences. She wrote under the pseudonym "Gul Makai," first in her native language of Urdu, and later in an English translation.

> "Since today was the last day of our school, we decided to play in the playground a bit longer. I am of the view that the school will one day reopen but while leaving I looked at the building as if I would not come here again."

Malala's first diary entry was published in 2009—about fifty years after Anne Frank's diary was published. The series was called "Diary of a Pakistani Schoolgirl," and the first entry was titled "I Am Afraid." In it, Malala described her nightmares, her fears, and her desire to keep going to class, despite the new rules forbidding girls from attending school. Her stories were published for ten weeks, and by sharing her personal experiences, Malala was able to give readers all over the world an intimate glimpse into a frightening reality. Her words were read by hundreds of thousands of people—including the violent men she was writing about.

Malala began to speak out publicly, advocating for girls' education and peace. This, combined with her diary entries, made her a threat to the Taliban—and a target. Three years after she published her first diaries, the Taliban sent several of their members to attack her. She was fourteen when she was shot in the head for daring to share her story. She survived the attack and has gone on to become a world-famous activist for girls around the world. In 2014, when she was just seventeen years old, Malala became the youngest person ever to win the Nobel Peace Prize.

THE PODGÓRSKI SISTERS

BORN IN LIPA, POLAND, 1925 (STEFANIA) AND 1935 (HELENA)

There are countless heroic tales of young people who did extraordinary things during World War II. One example comes from Poland, where Stefania Podgórski and her little sister, Helena, risked everything to save the lives of thirteen total strangers.

In 1942, sixteen-year-old Stefania and her six-year-old sister, Helena, lived in Przemyśl, a Nazi-controlled town. Their father had died, and their mother and brother had been forced into a German work camp. Stefania and Helena were Catholic, so they had some rights, including being able to rent their own apartment (many Catholic Poles were persecuted by the Nazis, which is why the girls' mother and brother had been sent away). All the Jews in town were forced to live in a ghetto (a small, heavily controlled area). Stefania knew this wasn't fair, and she would often sneak food into the ghetto to share with her former boss,

Mr. Diamant, and his family. Mr. Diamant had helped care for Stefania and Helena when their mother was sent away, and Stefania told him she would help his family if they ever needed it.

Soon word spread that the ghetto was being "liquidated," meaning that Jews were being put on trains and sent to death camps. One day there was a knock at Stefania's door: it was Max, Mr. Diamant's son. He had escaped the death camp train and needed a place to hide. Stefania was terrified, but she had promised the Diamants that she would help. Soon Max was able to bring the rest of his family; the group grew to thirteen in all. Again, Stefania was afraid. She knew if they were caught, they would *all* be killed. But she thought of her mother, who had taught her to care for all people. Stefania welcomed the thirteen people into her small, cramped attic.

Every day Stefania worked to collect enough food to feed everyone without arousing any suspicion. She had very little money, so she knitted sweaters and sold them or traded them for food. Little Helena did everyone's laundry, brought them water, and often ran dangerous errands because, as a child, she aroused less suspicion.

Stefania and Helena successfully hid the thirteen people in their home for two years, until the town was liberated. The Diamants were tired and weak but happy to be alive. And they owed their lives to the two brave sisters. Stefania turned eighteen soon after liberation, and Max proposed to her. They were married—and later moved to America and raised a family.

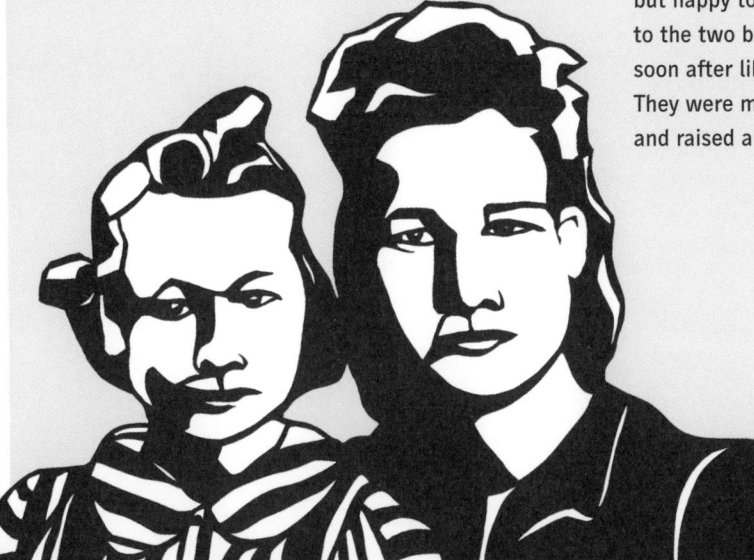

TRISHA PRABHU

BORN IN ARLINGTON HEIGHTS, ILLINOIS, 2000

She's the CEO of a fast-growing tech company, the first female youth governor of Illinois *and* she takes a full AP course load. Wait—*what?* Yes, Trisha Prabhu, CEO of ReThink, is a high school student. Despite all her achievements, Trisha describes herself as "a pretty average teenager" who likes to "go out with friends, read, and sleep a lot." When asked how she manages to fit it all in, Trisha says, "When you're the CEO of a company in high school, you really learn to time-manage."

It began in 2013, when thirteen-year-old Trisha heard a tragic story on the news: an eleven-year-old girl in Florida had committed suicide after being repeatedly cyberbullied. Trisha couldn't stop thinking about the girl. How could this have happened? And what could be done to prevent it from happening again?

Trisha began by doing research, and learned how widespread and dangerous cyberbullying is. Victims can suffer from depression, anxiety, and low self-esteem, and are at greater risk of dropping out of school. She also learned that many of the hurtful messages people send are composed and sent quickly, often on phones. Trisha wondered if there was a way to get people to pause and think for a minute before sending a potentially damaging text.

> "I really enjoy being a student, I really enjoy being the CEO, I enjoy being a teenager *and* a change maker."

And that's how Trisha came up with ReThink, an award-winning app that detects and stops cyberbullying and online hate before the damage is done. Trisha already knew how to code—she'd started when she was ten, and she often spent her school lunchtime learning about computers.

ReThink learns and detects thousands of the most common words and phrases used in cyberbullying. If you have it on your phone or device, it notices when you're about to send such a message. It doesn't delete it—instead, it asks if you *really* want to send the message. That way, the user gets a chance to pause, review, and think, *Hold on; am I sure I want to post that?*

Trisha's app has been downloaded hundreds of thousands of times, and she's expanded her company to also include antibullying curriculum used in more than thirteen hundred schools. The state of Michigan even adopted Trisha's materials for more than a million of its students. As part of the first generation to grow up with technology like smartphones and the internet, Trisha wants to use that technology for good, and ReThink is doing just that.

MARYAM MIRZAKHANI

When Maryam Mirzakhani was in sixth grade, she was interested in math, but she struggled with some of the concepts. Her teacher discouraged her, telling her she'd probably never be good at it. Maryam felt terrible and started to lose interest in math. That is, until the next year, when she had a wonderful teacher who helped rebuild her confidence. She also had a loyal best friend, Roya Beheshti, who saw how much joy Maryam got from math. Roya encouraged her friend not to give up on it. With this support, Maryam became excited about math again, and she soon soared to the top of the class.

Maryam and Roya remained best friends throughout middle school. They both loved browsing local bookstores, talking about math, and challenging each other to read and learn as much as possible.

When Maryam and Roya were in high school, they learned about a competition called the International Mathematical Olympiad. They decided they wanted to be part of it—even though their country of Iran had never had a girl on its team. They had no idea how well they'd do in the prestigious competition, but they wanted the opportunity to find out. They began by convincing the principal of their all-girls school that the school should be offering math and problem-solving classes like the ones offered at the all-boys school. While Maryam and Roya's school had math classes, they were nowhere near as advanced as the courses the boys got. The principal was supportive and agreed to improve the classes.

> **"It is invaluable to have a friend who shares your interests...It helps you stay motivated."**

In 1994, Maryam and Roya became the first Iranian girls to make the Mathematical Olympiad team. Maryam's score earned her a gold medal, and Roya received a silver medal. Maryam returned to the competition the next year and got a perfect score. She went on to study mathematics in college in Iran, and then at Harvard University in America. She began to be recognized by peers and professors as a true math genius, and was known for her determination and relentless curiosity. She always spoke up and asked questions, even though English was not her first language.

By age twenty-seven, Maryam was teaching math at Princeton, and then she became a professor at Stanford University. Roya also became a math professor, and they remained friends. In 2014 Maryam became the first woman (and the first Iranian) to win the Fields Medal (which is like the Academy Awards for Math). Sadly, Maryam's contributions to the world of mathematics were cut short just three years later, when she died of breast cancer at age forty.

ANDINI "ANN" MAKOSINSKI

BORN IN VICTORIA, BC, CANADA, 1997

Like most kids, Ann Makosinski loved to play with toys. But the toys she spent hours playing with were a bit unusual—and totally one of a kind. Ann's parents didn't buy her store-bought toys. Instead, they gave her materials like cardboard, tape, wire, and scraps of paper and encouraged her to make her own playthings. They weren't trying to be mean; they were encouraging her to use her imagination. And it worked. By age seven, Ann was inventing gadgets, machines, and toys. Her love for inventing grew into a love for all things scientific, and by the time she got to middle school she was enthusiastically entering science fairs every year.

Her big break came when she was fifteen, and she invented the Hollow Flashlight: a flashlight powered solely by body heat—no batteries. She got the idea when she heard about a problem: a friend of hers was living in the Philippines, and her family couldn't afford electricity. Because she couldn't study at night, she failed all of her classes at school. Ann knew there must be a solution. She remembered a previous science fair project where she'd used Peltier tiles, which produce electricity when one side is heated and the other is cooled. She thought about how those tiles could be used to power a flashlight. After many sketches, dead ends, do-overs, and prototypes, she finally figured it out. And the Hollow Flashlight took first place at the Google Science Fair.

Ann also invented the eDrink, a coffee cup that charges your phone with the excess heat of your beverage. The idea for it came from two common problems that Ann saw on her high school campus: everyone's phone batteries were always low, and people had to wait a long time while their too-hot coffee cooled. She combined the two and came up with an innovation.

> **"I'm not the best in my class and I probably never will be, but I can think and I can solve problems when I see them."**

Ann has a popular YouTube channel, where she talks about everything from her cat to her favorite old-fashioned movie stars to her latest inventions. She clearly loves science, but she surprised some people when she decided to study English literature in college. "But Ann," they asked, "what about science?" Ann just laughed—she thinks it's silly that people assume you can love only one kind of learning. A *true* scientist is fascinated by all aspects of the world around her, and Ann wants to learn about all of it.

MARIA MITCHELL

Maria Mitchell, the first female astronomer in America, is known for discovering a comet. Her love for science, the stars, and the vast night sky began at an early age, when she was growing up in the whaling village of Nantucket.

Maria was the third of eleven children. She was raised in a Quaker community, which was unique at the time for its commitment to treating men and women, boys and girls equally. In many other parts of the country, education for girls was not a priority. But that was not the case in the Mitchell home or in their broader Quaker community, where women had great independence and access to education.

> **"We especially need imagination in science. It is not all mathematics, nor all logic, but it is somewhat beauty and poetry."**

From the time she was quite young, Maria was an avid learner. Her father was a teacher and an astronomer, and he noted her interest in the sciences early on. Maria had exceptional vision, great patience, and incredible attention to detail—all qualities needed to be an astronomer, and all qualities that came in very handy on the long nights she spent with her father in his observatory, assisting him in his work and developing her own science skills.

Their most exciting collaboration came when Maria was about twelve, and she and her father observed and charted the course of a solar eclipse (when the moon comes between Earth and the sun). The eclipse was a huge

deal; Mr. Mitchell had been preparing for it for years, and all the newspapers reported on the rare event. On February 19, 1829, Maria and her father set up their telescopes and waited for the eclipse. Maria held a chronometer on her lap and carefully counted the seconds while Mr. Mitchell watched the eclipse. Together they were able to calculate the exact moment of "first contact"— when the edge of the moon first crosses the edge of the sun—and it would not have happened without Maria. She wasn't just an assistant, or a kid whose dad allowed her to watch him work. She was an astronomer—a real scientist—and the experience set her on her life path.

When Maria was fourteen, local whalers began to hire her to do complex navigational computations for their whaling journeys. She then became a librarian, and she educated herself further by reading every book in the library. At seventeen, she started her own school—it was open to white *and* black students, which was very rare at that time. She went on to discover a comet before she turned thirty and became one of the top scientists of her time.

JAZZ JENNINGS

JAZZ JENNINGS IS a typical American teenager. She loves soccer, mermaids, and hanging out with her friends. She's a good student and a member of student government. She gets moody and insecure but can also be silly and crazy. Unlike most teenage girls, though, Jazz is the star of her own reality TV show. She's also transgender, meaning that she was assigned male at birth but has been a girl since she or anyone else can remember.

Jazz and her family went public with her story in 2007, when Jazz was just six years old. After months of debate and consultation with psychiatrists, television producers, and family members, Jazz's parents agreed to be interviewed by journalist Barbara Walters for the popular TV show *20/20*. Jazz's parents knew that many people would be outraged because they didn't understand or approve of parents raising a transgender child. But that's exactly why they chose to go public—to help people understand. They knew how hard life can be for transgender children and their families, and they wanted to show the world what it looks like to love and respect people of all gender identities.

From the moment she could communicate, Jazz made it clear that she was a girl. As a baby, she would unsnap her onesies to make them look like dresses. She wore her big sister's dress-up clothes, and loved putting on glitter and makeup and playing with dolls. But it was more than that. She would correct anyone who referred to her as a boy. If her dad said "Good boy," she'd quickly say "Good *girl!*" Jazz's parents assumed it was something she'd grow out of, but as time passed, it only became more intense.

It's important to recognize that many children are fluid with their gender identities. Lots of young boys play with dolls and like to wear dresses and pink clothes. And many girls grow up loving "boy things." A child who prefers the clothing, colors, activities, gestures, and hairstyles associated with the opposite sex is not automatically transgender. Who said that only boys can play with trucks and trains? Who said that princess dresses are just for girls?

> "Not only do we all deserve to be loved, but we deserve to love ourselves for who we are. I want to live in a world where everyone has the freedom to be their authentic self."

The turning point for Jazz's mom came when two-year-old Jazz asked when the "Good Fairy" was going to come with her "magic wand." The fairy, Jazz explained, was going to transform her genitals from male to female. Her mother was shocked; she had no idea where her child would get an idea like this. In her book *I Am Jazz*, Jazz explains that the idea of the fairy came from an incredibly vivid dream she had. When she woke up she was convinced it was real, and she was thrilled. She was devastated when her mom explained that there was no fairy who could do that.

Jazz had no examples of transgender people in her life. She wasn't copying anyone, and her parents weren't forcing her to act a certain way. She didn't even know there was a word for how she felt. It wasn't right or wrong, good or bad. Jazz just knew that she was born with a boy body but had "a girl brain," as she often explained it. By the time Jazz was four, her mom believed that something truly different was happening, and she took Jazz to see a specialist in gender identity. Jazz was diagnosed with what was then still termed a disorder—Gender Identity Disorder—becoming the youngest person on record to receive the diagnosis.

Her parents allowed her to live as a girl at home, but outside of the house, including at preschool, Jazz wore gender-neutral clothes—no dresses. Her parents kept her hair short and used male pronouns like "he" and "his." At her preschool recital, Jazz cried because she wasn't allowed to wear leotards, tights, and tutus like the other girls. It wasn't that Jazz's parents disapproved of who she was; they were trying to protect their child, because they knew that many people would not respond well to their "boy" walking around dressed like a girl. They wanted to protect Jazz, but they soon realized that to truly protect her, they needed to fully accept and support her.

As Jazz's parents learned more about transgender youth and gender identity, they came across a very serious statistic: about 50 percent of people under age twenty who identify as transgender try to commit suicide. This is often in response to bullying and/or rejection by family. Supporting Jazz and allowing her to transition was not just a lifestyle choice, they realized. It was a matter of life and death.

Just before her fifth birthday, Jazz's parents sat the family down and explained to her older brothers, sister, and grandparents that Jazz was a girl. She would use "she" and "her" pronouns, grow her hair out, and dress as she pleased. They allowed Jazz to wear a one-piece bathing suit at her fifth birthday party, and that fall she started kindergarten with her girl name and pronouns. Jazz was the happiest they'd ever seen her.

For the next several years, Jazz was a normal kid attending school and playing soccer—and also working as a spokesperson and advocate for trans youth. After the *20/20* episode, Jazz helped start the TransKids Purple Rainbow Foundation, to assist other transgender youth. A documentary about them appeared on Oprah Winfrey's network, and Jazz wrote a children's book and a best-selling memoir. When Jazz was fourteen, the family agreed to film a season of *I Am Jazz*, a docuseries that would bring Jazz and the family into the national spotlight once again. Jazz agreed to do it not because she craved the attention or wanted to be a superstar but because she wanted to continue to have an impact and tell a story that needs to be told.

The groundbreaking show has enabled millions of viewers of all ages to understand and experience the joys and challenges of Jazz's life. The show captures Jazz and her friends and family enjoying fun everyday moments, but it also shows the struggles that Jazz faces: the bullying, the online harassment, the kids (and adults) who don't get it. It also shows the complex decisions that Jazz and her family must make about her body and medical hormone and surgical treatments. Puberty can be a challenging time for most teenagers, but for transgender youth it's especially difficult.

There have been many times when Jazz and her family doubted their decision to make their lives so public. What makes it worthwhile is the feedback, especially from young lesbian, gay, bisexual, transgender, and queer (LGBTQ) people who say that Jazz has helped them come out to their parents and even saved their lives. By allowing the public to get to know her and her family, Jazz gets to show millions of viewers that she is who she is. And that's a girl named Jazz.

JANET MOCK

BORN IN HONOLULU, HAWAII, 1983

Janet Mock ran for class treasurer at the end of her ninth-grade year at her public high school in Honolulu, Hawaii, and she won. At the beginning of the next school year, she took the stage in the school cafeteria with the other newly elected members of student government for a back-to-school assembly. The class officers introduced themselves, one by one. When it was Janet's turn, she greeted her three hundred fellow sophomores with "I'm Janet, your class treasurer!" She thanked them for their votes and their support, and stepped back.

> "I believe that telling our stories, first to ourselves and then to one another and the world, is a revolutionary act."

For Janet this was *huge*. When she ran for class treasurer, the name on the ballot was her birth name, the one her parents gave her when they perceived her to be a boy. During the summer before tenth grade, Janet made the transition from the boy everyone saw her as to the girl she had always known herself to be. For a mixed-race transgender girl who'd grown up in poverty without trans role models, this was not an easy thing to do. Luckily she had the support of her best friend, Wendi, who encouraged Janet to be her true self.

When they met, the first thing Wendi said to Janet was, "Are you *ma'hu*?" *Ma'hu* is a gender role in traditional Hawaiian society that refers to people who exhibit both feminine and masculine traits. It roughly translates as someone who is in-between genders, and before Hawaii was colonized in the nineteenth century, *ma'hu* people were well respected. Now *ma'hu* is often used as a slur against gay men, but many trans and gender-nonconforming Hawaiians are reclaiming the term in a positive way. When Wendi asked Janet if she was *ma'hu*, Janet said "No!" She was still scared to admit her truth, but inside, she was thrilled that Wendi could see who she really was.

Janet's appearance on that stage was a public coming-out to her peers. She was unapologetic about who she was, and for the most part, her peers and the school's staff supported her. One teacher was openly dismissive. She repeatedly misgendered Janet, calling her "him" and "he" and using her birth name instead of "Janet" while taking roll each day. While this may not seem like a big deal to some people, names are important parts of our identities.

Janet went on to become a successful journalist, author of two books, and television personality who regularly shares her story and advocates for feminism, racial justice, and LGBTQ rights. And she is still close with her dear friend Wendi.

51

AMANDLA STENBERG

AMANDLA STENBERG WAS DETERMINED
to get the part. The movie was based on her favorite books, and she just knew she could play the character of Rue, the brave young girl in *The Hunger Games*. She wanted to stand out at her audition, so she put on old clothes, rolled in the dirt in her backyard, and filled her hair with twigs and leaves. She showed up to her audition at the director's house looking like she'd been living in the woods for weeks, just like Rue's character in the books. And it worked! Eleven-year-old Amandla got the role, and soon she was on the film set, meeting famous actors like Jennifer Lawrence and getting strapped into harnesses so she could do crazy stunts just like daring little Rue.

When the first *Hunger Games* movie came out, it was a huge box-office success. Amandla won rave reviews for her bold, emotional portrayal of Rue. But not everyone thought Amandla—who is mixed race, with a black mother and a white father—should be playing Rue. Soon she was being attacked on social media by people who didn't think Rue should be black. Even though *The Hunger Games* author Suzanne Collins specifies that Rue has "dark brown skin and eyes," there were a lot of people who just couldn't handle it. They took to Twitter, Instagram, Tumblr, and Facebook to complain. Some people took it far, calling Amandla terrible racist names. It was a harsh introduction to the limelight, and it was also a very personal introduction to racism for her. Amandla had been in the public eye since she got her first gig at age four, as a model for a Disney catalog. She'd appeared in commercials, films, and videos throughout her childhood. But *The Hunger Games* was her biggest role by far, and these nasty fan reactions showed her that

no matter what she did, her race would be a factor for her entire career. She didn't let this intimidate her, though—in fact, it motivated her to become a strong, outspoken activist.

> "There are so many different ways to make art. And so many good stories. You don't have to have a budget. I feel like it's super possible these days for people to make anything, no matter who you are or where you come from."

The next time Amandla made waves online, it wasn't because of a new movie or high-profile Hollywood project—it was because of a school project. Amandla and a classmate made a video about black women's hair and cultural appropriation as an assignment for their tenth-grade history class. The video is called "Don't Cash Crop My Cornrows," and in it Amandla offers a succinct explanation of cultural appropriation. She explains why it can be problematic when white people—especially celebrities—adopt aspects of black culture but fail to show concern for problems that black communities face. She calls out specific celebrities who have emulated hip hop culture and then remained silent during times of crisis, and asks the question, "What if America loved black people as much as black culture?" In addition to presenting the video in class, Amandla and her friend shared it on Tumblr. Amandla already had a lot of followers there, and the school-project video went viral.

The response to the video was enormous, and Amandla did a lot of interviews with major media outlets. She talked openly about race and racism, as well as gender and sexuality. She got positive feedback from people who were glad to see her using her social-media platform to speak on important issues. But, once again, she was also subject to negative backlash. She wasn't opposed to people disagreeing with her, but she did have a hard time with the cruel and ignorant comments she received. Some people warned that if she kept speaking up about issues like race and gender it might jeopardize her acting career. Amandla had a choice to make: would she continue speaking on the internet about these things that she used to speak about only with her friends and family and classmates? Or would she keep those ideas to herself?

Amandla decided that if she didn't talk about the things she cared about, she wouldn't be presenting her true self, even though presenting your true self isn't always easy. She continued to speak about race and identity, including her own gender identity and sexuality, which she describes as fluid—she doesn't always feel like a girl *or* a boy, and she has written and shared her thoughts on what it means to be a young person exploring these complex concepts.

> "I feel like we forget that we're all very human, and social media is a way to break down divides between us."

Presenting your true self means taking risks and being willing to be vulnerable. But it also means being honest and true, and potentially inspiring others to do the same. Amandla knows that as a celebrity, she has a built-in platform that she can use to reach many young people who might feel silenced or ashamed about who they are. And while social media can be used in negative ways, it can also create powerful connections.

Amandla also knows that there's a huge amount of pressure on her to always say the "right" thing or represent the "right" point of view. She accepts this and wants to use social media to actually *do something*—to impact culture and connect with others. The more she hears from young people who have been inspired and empowered by her words and actions, the more she knows she's doing the right thing.

Acting is not Amandla's only artistic outlet— she also sings, plays violin, and directs and edits music videos. She appeared in Beyoncé's groundbreaking video project *Lemonade* and in films like *Everything, Everything* and *The Hate U Give*. She interviewed the feminist icon Gloria Steinem, and she was handpicked by Oprah Winfrey to give a keynote speech for Oprah's *Super Soul Sunday*.

Oh, and she also writes comics! Amandla is the author of the *Niobe* series, the first internationally distributed comic book series to be written by a black woman, illustrated by a black artist, and to feature a black main character (a magical teenage elf who looks *a lot* like Amandla). Amandla grew up loving sci-fi and fantasy books like *The Lord of the Rings* trilogy, and she always wished for characters who felt more like her. Working on *Niobe* was a way to make that happen.

Amandla is by no means alone in her role as a high-profile young person who uses her platform for positive change. She's part of a generation of people who, as she says, are "wicked smart" and have grown up "with computers in their hands"—and who are working hard to use those assets in smart, powerful, and empowering ways.

MARLEY DIAS

BORN IN WEST ORANGE, NEW JERSEY, 2003

Eleven-year-old Marley Dias loved to read. She loved getting lost in a great story, imagining new worlds, and learning new things. But the more books she read, the more she noticed that most of the main characters, especially in classic books, were boys: mostly white boys, and sometimes, white boys with dogs. Marley didn't mind reading about boys and dogs (or wizards or unicorns or fairies), but as a young black girl, she also wanted to see someone like herself as the main character. She wanted to imagine *herself* as the hero.

> **"You don't have to be very old to start trying to fix the problems you see in the world around you."**

Marley decided to do something about it. She began by doing research to see if anyone else had noticed this problem. She learned that less than 10 percent of children's books published in 2015 had a black person as the main character. And of 3,400 children's books published that year, fewer than 100 were about Latino characters. And even though children's books have gradually become more diverse, many libraries have only older books that don't reflect this shift.

Diversity in books benefits everyone: it gives us a broader understanding of who we are as a nation, and a world. Almost half of the children in the United States are children of color, so why should almost all the books be about white kids? Marley wanted more diverse books to be available for everyone, so she started a campaign to collect and donate a thousand books about black girls, so more girls like herself would have access to books that reflected their experiences.

She was excited about her new idea, but *how* exactly would she get all those books? She decided to use social media and spread her message with the hashtag #1000BlackGirlBooks. And it worked.

> **"Frustration is fuel that can lead to the development of an innovative and useful idea."**

Within months, Marley's campaign got the attention of writers, librarians, booksellers, and other people across the country, and the books began pouring in. Journalists wrote stories about her, and soon Marley had more than four thousand books to donate!

She had exceeded her goal, but Marley was just getting started. She continued to collect books (up to nearly ten thousand!), created a resource guide for educators, and used her newfound media attention to speak to broad audiences about the importance of diversity in kids' books. She even got to interview Hillary Clinton and edit her own online zine for *Elle* magazine. And eventually, the girl who loved books got to write and publish her *own* book—a guide to activism—when she was just twelve years old.

ELIZABETH COTTEN

BORN IN CARRBORO, NORTH CAROLINA, 1895

Elizabeth Cotten was seven years old when she began teaching herself to play banjo by borrowing her big brother's instruments when he wasn't home. She had heard many traditional folk songs from her family, including her grandparents, who were both freed slaves. Since she was left-handed, Elizabeth would flip her brother's banjo upside down and play it in reverse, playing bass with her fingers and the melody with her thumb. She didn't know it then, but she'd developed a completely unique style of playing that would become known as "Cotten picking," because of the way she "picked" the guitar strings to create melodies.

Elizabeth's brother left home when she was nine, taking his instruments with him. Desperate to keep playing, Elizabeth began working as a domestic (another name for a maid) for a neighbor, where she earned seventy-five cents a month. She eventually saved enough money to buy her very own guitar—it cost $3.75, and it meant the world to her. By the time she was eleven, she was composing her own songs, including one that would later become her most famous, "Freight Train" (about the loud trains that kept her awake at night). She played and wrote songs constantly until she was fifteen, when she got married, had a daughter, and was advised by her pastor to play only "church songs." Back then, women were expected to be polite wives and mothers—not musicians.

Elizabeth didn't pick up a guitar again for more than forty years, when she was working as a domestic for a family and began playing one of their guitars. That family happened to be the well-known family of musicians, the Seegers, which included singers Pete and Mike Seeger. They were in awe of the talent she'd kept hidden, and with their support, Elizabeth recorded her first album and began performing concerts. She was well into her sixties when she finally gained recognition, but it was the songs she'd written as a child that made the most impact. Elizabeth Cotten's original songs, like "Freight Train," "Shake Sugaree," and "Goin' Down the Road Feelin' Bad," have been covered by musicians like Bob Dylan, Joan Baez, the Grateful Dead, and many more.

ESG

The Scroggins sisters grew up in a rough neighborhood. To keep her young daughters off the streets, Helen Scroggins agreed to buy them instruments, but she couldn't afford to pay for lessons. So the teenage sisters—Renee, Marie, Valerie, and Deborah—decided to figure out how to play music themselves.

With Deborah on bass, Marie on congas and vocals, Renee on guitar, and Valerie on drums, they learned popular songs by artists like Chaka Khan and the Rolling Stones by watching TV and listening to their mom's records. They performed for their mom every Friday evening to prove that they were actually practicing. As they got better, they decided to stop playing other people's music and write their own. They were inspired by the funk of James Brown and the Jackson 5, the rhythms of disco, and the sounds of their neighborhood, including the percussive Latin music played in local parks and a new kind of music known as hip hop.

They called themselves ESG (which stands for "emerald, sapphire, and gold"), and the songs they developed were totally unique—and really, really good. They entered a talent contest at a local record store, and soon they were playing at New York City punk, disco, and hip hop clubs. They got a record deal, made several albums, and played concerts with bands like The Clash and Grandmaster Flash. Eventually, Deborah left the band, and the sisters invited other musicians to play with them.

One of the most notable things about ESG is that their songs have been sampled by hundreds (if not thousands) of other bands, meaning that artists take portions of their rhythms and use them to create new songs. Their song "UFO" has been sampled by everyone from Public Enemy to Nas to Nine Inch Nails. Unfortunately, most people haven't obtained permission to use the samples, and the Scroggins sisters haven't gotten the credit or money they deserve. And most people still don't realize that many of their favorite rap songs are built on the music of teenage girls!

LORDE

BORN IN TAKAPUNA, NEW ZEALAND, 1996

Her real name is Ella Marija Lani Yelich-O'Connor, but the rest of the world knows her as Lorde, the groundbreaking girl who went from being a teenager in a tiny New Zealand town to an international pop star seemingly overnight. Lorde was signed to a record label at age twelve, started writing songs when she was around fourteen, and released her first few songs at age sixteen, when her single "Royals" became an international hit.

Lorde is known for her pop songs, but don't just call her a *singer*—she's a writer, musician, and producer who works hard to craft unique songs with expressive lyrics. She credits her mom, a poet, for encouraging her love of language by constantly giving her new books to read. The

books Lorde read as a child inspired her to write stories of her own—and those stories eventually influenced her song lyrics. At first she didn't really know how to write songs, but she kept at it until it started to make sense.

She released her first EP, *The Love Club*, online for free because she wanted people her age to be able to access the music. It was downloaded by sixty thousand people before it was picked up by a music label, and within a few months, her song "Royals" was a #1 hit around the world. Lorde's stardom happened quickly—when she flew to New York City to perform for the first time, it was her first time ever on an airplane. Just one year after self-releasing her EP, her full-length album, *Heroine*, came out. And she won two Grammys!

It took Lorde three years to create, record, and release her next full-length album. She felt a lot of pressure to hurry up and make more hit songs, but she took her time and didn't care if people were annoyed. She wanted to make music she loved and believed in, and when she finally released *Melodrama* in 2017, her fans—and the critics—were not disappointed.

SELENA

BORN IN LAKE JACKSON, TEXAS, 1971

Selena Quintanilla's life as a performer began when she was very young. Her father was a musician, and he enjoyed teaching Selena's older siblings how to play music. When she was three years old, Selena got mad that she was being left out and insisted that her dad teach her about music, too. She would sing songs she heard on the radio, and her father noticed that she had an amazing voice—and perfect pitch. He was convinced she'd be a star. When Selena was eight, the Quintanilla family fell on hard times and decided to rely on their talents. They formed a band and toured around Texas in an old van, playing any gig they could get. They played Tejano music, a popular upbeat style of Latin music that blends the rhythms of Texas and Mexican music (also known as "Tex-Mex"), American pop, and polka. Selena was the lead singer, and within a few years, she was Tejano's biggest superstar.

When Selena was fifteen, she won a Tejano Music Award for female vocalist and performer of the year, and her career took off. She was an instantly beloved pop star who was able to cross over between American and Mexican audiences. One challenge for Selena was that all her songs were in Spanish—but she spoke only English! She took intensive Spanish lessons so she could communicate with her new fan base, but she always sang with a Texas accent. Her songs contained traditional Tejano elements, but Selena also incorporated contemporary pop music and disco into her music as well. Even her outfits reflected her dynamic identity: she'd wear traditional Mexican-style bolero jackets with cowboy boots and leather miniskirts. In the male-dominated world of Tejano music, Selena was a true rebel. She released her first full-length album at age seventeen, and her fourth album, *Amor Prohibido* ("Forbidden Love"), is considered one of the best Latin music records of all time.

Selena was the biggest Latin music star until her untimely death at age twenty-three, when she was shot and killed by the president of her fan club. The tragic loss sent shockwaves through many communities, and more than sixty thousand mourners attended the funeral to pay tribute to their beloved Selena.

LORELLA PRAELI

BORN IN ICA, PERU, 1988

WHEN LORELLA PRAELI WAS a child, she used to fall down *all* the time. Walking was especially difficult for her—she'd been hit by a car when she was just two years old, and her right leg was so badly damaged that doctors had to remove it. Lorella learned to get around with crutches, and a prosthetic leg, but it wasn't easy. Each time she fell, everyone around her (even strangers on the street) would rush to help her up—everyone, that is, except her father. Was it because he was mean and didn't want to help his daughter? No—it was because he wanted her to learn a valuable lesson.

"Thank you," he would tell those eager to help Lorella stand, "but she can do it on her own."

And she would. Again and again, Lorella used her strength and determination to get back up—and to this day she credits her father for helping her gain the confidence and courage to succeed.

> "What says the most about who you are is your ability to get back up and fight."

When Lorella's accident occurred, her family was living in their native country of Peru. Once her leg was amputated, she required years of medical attention. The specialists she needed to see were all in America, so after years of traveling back and forth, her parents made a difficult decision: Lorella, her sister, and her mom would move to Connecticut to live with family, Lorella's father joined them for a year and then moved back to Peru.

Lorella was ten years old when they arrived in the United States. Life in Connecticut was *very* different from life in Peru, but Lorella adjusted

well, learning English quickly and doing great in school. She loved making friends, but it wasn't easy. The people in her new town were mostly white, and Lorella was a brown-skinned, Spanish-speaking girl with one leg. The teasing began in middle school.

The cruelest bullying happened online. People called her "peg leg," "border hopper," and worse. She didn't know what to do. She didn't want to tell her mom, because she didn't want to stress her out, so Lorella decided to deal with it herself. She printed screenshots of the bullying and went right to her school officials with a big stack of evidence. She calmly explained what had been happening and asked the school to help her. And they did. The girl behind the bullying was identified, and she apologized to Lorella. Even though Lorella's feelings were deeply hurt, she forgave the girl and decided to move on.

But the bullying still haunted her. In ninth grade Lorella learned about a special all-day anti-bullying program sponsored by the Anti-Defamation League (ADL). It was offered to tenth graders, but Lorella knew she wanted to be involved. She contacted the coordinator and asked if she could participate. She ended up sharing her story with the entire tenth-grade class. She talked about being bullied, as well as what it was like to be an immigrant with a visible disability. She felt vulnerable and nervous, but she also felt empowered. Her story was special, and it made an impact on her peers. If Lorella could survive a terrible accident, learn how to walk with one leg, move to a new country, learn a new language, and *still* have the strength to stand up for herself and speak out, then anyone could!

With this in mind, she contacted the ADL and asked, boldly: "Is there anything else I can do?" They said *yes*—and she spent the rest of her high school days running the Names Can Really Hurt Us Program and speaking out against bullying whenever she could, whether at a conference in New York City or at the Connecticut state legislature.

But Lorella's story of perseverance and courage doesn't end there. During her senior year of high school, she was thrilled to begin filling out college applications. When a financial aid form asked for her Social Security number, Lorella asked her mom for this basic information. That's when her mom delivered life-changing news.

"Lorella," she told her nervously, "we are undocumented. You are not an American citizen." Suddenly, it all made sense—*that* was why Lorella's aunt was always the one to fill out the forms for apartment rentals, cell phone contracts, and water and electric bills. *That* was why Lorella's mom, who had been a psychiatrist in Peru, could only find work cleaning houses in America. Lorella understood—but she was also terrified. Would she be able to go to college? Would she get arrested? Deported? She was afraid, but she had fought too hard to find her place in America to give up now.

So she kept applying, but didn't check the box that asked if she was a citizen. She was accepted and enrolled into college, but now she carried a huge secret. She had learned to live with confidence as a one-legged, brown-skinned girl in America—but now she felt a new kind of shame. Who was she? She *felt* American—but she wasn't *legal*. The words "illegal" and "alien" were embarrassing—and hurtful.

Lorella was very politically active, and she knew how controversial the topic of immigration was. She knew how harshly people like her family were often judged. And she knew that

there was a chance she might get deported and sent back to Peru. So she told no one. She campaigned for Barack Obama in 2008, excelled in her classes, and even won a prestigious fellowship. But she also felt weighed down by this secret. Finally, when she was twenty, a close friend asked her what was wrong, and she confessed.

"I'm undocumented," she said, terrified of how he would react.

"So what?" he asked. "You're *Lorella*, with or without papers."

Lorella was flooded with relief. She was aware that a pro–immigrant rights movement was growing, and that many young people were organizing and encouraging the newly elected President Obama to sign legislation to help young undocumented immigrants. These young activists were known as Dreamers, and Lorella was ready to become one. At age twenty-one, she contacted United We Dream (UWD), the largest immigrant youth–led organization in America, and told them, "I am so sick of hiding and not sharing my story." She was immediately connected to many young people who were unashamed of their undocumented status.

Soon after, Lorella spoke at a press conference in Connecticut. She walked onto a stage in front of a huge crowd, not unlike that room of tenth graders she'd faced back in high school. There, she told her story in public for the first time. "The power and the beauty of coming out of the shadows," she told the crowd, "is that you can't go back." And she never did.

Using all of the skills she'd honed over the years, Lorella went on to become a major leader with UWD, even meeting with President Obama himself. And remember that friend who supported her when she confessed her immigration status? They got married, and Lorella Praeli became an American citizen.

SOPHIE CRUZ

Five-year-old Sophie Cruz became one of America's youngest immigration rights activists when she delivered a powerful message to Pope Francis. During his visit to Washington, DC, in 2015, Sophie ran up to the pope and gave him a letter she'd written. It read: "My heart is sad. I would like to ask you to speak with the president and Congress in legalizing my parents because every day I am scared that they will take them away from me."

Sophie was born in America, but her parents weren't: they came from Oaxaca, Mexico, escaping violence and poverty. Because they weren't American citizens, they could be deported at any time. Her bravery made an impact: the next morning Pope Francis addressed Congress and discussed immigration policy at length, asking them to treat immigrants "with the same compassion with which we want to be treated." Soon after, Sophie was invited to the White House, where she got to meet President Obama. In January 2017, Sophie was the youngest person to speak at the Women's March in Washington, DC. In both English and Spanish, she told the massive crowd, "Let us fight with love, faith, and courage so that our families will not be destroyed!"

BORN IN SAN ANTONIO, TEXAS, 1916

EMMA TENAYUCA

Emma Tenayuca was the second of eleven children. Her grandfather helped her read the newspaper every day and often took her to a local plaza where people hung around and talked politics. Young Emma, who would come to be known as *La Pasionaria* ("the passionate one"), absorbed the stories of what these Mexican-American workers faced: discrimination, beatings by the border patrol, and even deportation if they complained.

Emma's first arrest came in 1933, when she was just sixteen, after she joined a picket line of four hundred women workers at a cigar factory. The women were paid less than twenty cents an hour and treated cruelly by their bosses. Even though she didn't work there, Emma joined the fight.

After the cigar strike Emma began attending every protest in the area. She helped struggling workers and gave powerful speeches in English and Spanish. After she graduated from high school she helped form several unions of female workers, and by the time she was twenty she had been elected to a leadership position in a major union.

RUBY BRIDGES

RUBY BRIDGES WAS BORN in the same year that the United States Supreme Court voted to end segregation in schools. The ruling in that landmark case, *Brown vs. the Board of Education of Topeka*, declared that laws allowing separate schools for white and black students were unconstitutional.

Even though the law changed, many cities, counties, and states were slow to integrate, keeping black and white children in separate schools. And some outright refused to change. Six years after the court case, Ruby entered kindergarten in New Orleans, Louisiana. The school district was still segregated, so Ruby attended the all-black school. As was almost always the case, the schools for white students were far better than the schools for black students. They had nicer facilities, much more money, and better training for teachers. Toward the end of Ruby's kindergarten year, the federal government ordered the New Orleans school district to integrate.

Though a court case can change the law, it can't change people's feelings or behavior, and this case did *not* end racism. The school district agreed to integrate, but black students who wanted to enroll in the previously all-white schools first had to take a test to prove that they were "academically ready." Ruby was one of six children (all girls) who passed the test. Ruby's father wanted her to stay at the all-black school because he feared for her safety. But Ruby's mother wanted her daughter to receive the best education possible and attend William Frantz Elementary, which was just blocks from their home. Ruby's father finally agreed.

On the day of integration, November 14, 1960, Ruby and her mother drove to her new school. Ruby wore a special new dress and had nice white ribbons in her two braids. Her parents had told her she was going to a new school, and that she must behave. Ruby and her mother weren't alone on their short trip to Frantz Elementary: they were escorted by four federal marshals (a kind of law enforcement) who had been assigned by the federal government to protect them. Many white people in New Orleans were furious about integration and vowed to stop it from happening. Young Ruby didn't know who the marshals were, or why she needed protection. She didn't know that she was "integrating" a school, and she had no idea that many local white people were rushing to Frantz Elementary to stop her from coming to "their" school.

When they pulled up to the school, Ruby saw huge crowds of people. They were screaming and shouting. Some waved signs, and some were throwing things. Ruby's mother was terrified, and she clutched her daughter's hand tightly. Still, Ruby was too young to understand what was happening—she'd grown up in New Orleans and was used to big wild crowds. At first she thought they were celebrating Mardi Gras! But once they began walking through the crowd, she realized these people weren't happy. They weren't celebrating. They were angry. At *her*. Ruby didn't cry. She marched toward her new school, excited to start first grade.

Ruby spent the first day sitting quietly in the principal's office with her mother because the white protesters were causing such chaos, and parents were pulling their children out of school. On the second day, Ruby and her mother returned with the four marshals. The crowd was still there, hoping to intimidate them. Again, Ruby held her head high and went to school. This time she and her mother went into a classroom, where they were joined by one other person: Mrs. Barbara Henry, the only teacher in the entire school who was willing to teach a black child.

Mrs. Henry was a white woman from Boston, and she was new to Frantz Elementary. Unlike her colleagues, she was committed to education for all children. Ruby had never seen a white teacher before, and because Mrs. Henry looked a lot like the angry white women yelling at her outside, she didn't trust her right away. But Mrs. Henry was warm and caring, and she worked to distract Ruby from the hateful things happening at the school. Ruby realized that Mrs. Henry was a safe person who was there to help her.

On the third day of school, Ruby's mother went home, and it was just Ruby and Mrs. Henry in the classroom. It would be like that every single day for the rest of the school year. Mrs. Henry taught Ruby as if she were teaching an entire class. Ruby raised her hand, asked questions, and learned to read and write just as if she were in a normal classroom full of students.

Every morning Mrs. Henry would stand at the classroom window and watch Ruby come to school. She wanted to make sure no one hurt her. One day she saw Ruby stop in the middle of the crowd. Angry adults surrounded her, and it looked like Ruby was talking to them. Mrs. Henry was worried, and when Ruby came into class she asked what had happened. Ruby explained that she was praying for them. She said that every day she stopped a few blocks from school to say a prayer for the angry people, in hopes that they'd find love in their hearts. On this day, she'd forgotten to say the prayer before she got to school, so she stopped

in front of everyone to say it. Mrs. Henry was amazed at the courage and faith of this six-year-old girl.

Ruby did not have any friends that year, and she spent most lunches and recesses in the classroom with Mrs. Henry. The federal marshals stood watch at the classroom door and even escorted Ruby to and from the restroom. Ruby had nightmares, and after some people threatened to poison her food, she often refused to eat lunch. But she didn't complain, she did all her schoolwork, and she didn't miss a single day of school all year.

The backlash wasn't just limited to the protesting crowds at the school: Ruby's father lost his job, and the grocery store refused to sell food to her mother. Ruby's grandparents were sharecroppers, and they were forced to leave the land where they'd lived for twenty-five years. All of this cruelty was an attempt to intimidate the family and get them to take Ruby out of the school. But the Bridges family stayed strong—they knew this was about much more than just one child. They knew they were making history.

Ruby made it through the year and returned to Frantz Elementary for second grade. Many of the white families who had pulled their children from the school eventually allowed them to return. But the angry mobs didn't return—they realized that Ruby and her family weren't going to give up. Life for the Bridges family was still a challenge, but Ruby finished elementary school and went on to attend an integrated high school. She grew up and raised a family, and to this day she remains committed to working for civil rights and social justice.

Ruby Bridges has become a powerful symbol of courage in the face of hatred and racism.

BARBARA ROSE JOHNS

BORN IN NEW YORK, NEW YORK, 1935

"Well, why don't you do something about it?" Those were the words that sixteen-year-old Barbara Rose Johns's teacher spoke to her one day in the fall of 1950. Barbara was expressing her frustrations about the terrible conditions of Moton High School, her all-black segregated school in Farmville, Virginia. Moton was made to hold 180 students, but 450 were enrolled. Classes were crammed together, and some were even taught in old school buses. They had no gym, no cafeteria, no science labs, and no indoor plumbing. And the all-white school nearby? It had all those things, and more. And Barbara was sick of it.

Many faculty members and parents had been trying for years to get a new school built, but the all-white school board ignored them. When Barbara heard her teacher's response, she felt ignored too. *Do something about it . . .* she couldn't get those words out of her head, and she soon realized that her teacher wasn't ignoring her—she was motivating her to take action! Barbara was a determined young woman who came from a family that valued education and equality. By winter, Barbara had an idea: the entire student body should go on strike and demand a new school. And she would be the one to make it happen.

Barbara began by forming a secret committee of four trusted students with whom she shared her idea. By spring, they'd formed a larger strike committee of fifteen students, each with different ties to student communities. Barbara was the leader, but everyone played an important role.

Finally the day came. The principal received a phone call reporting that two students were ditching school. The call was a trick to get him off campus, and it worked. Once he'd left, messages were sent to every classroom, telling teachers to bring classes to the auditorium for an emergency assembly.

> **"There wasn't any fear. I just thought, 'this is your moment; seize it!'"**

Once all 450 students were in the room, the committee stepped forward from behind a curtain. They led everyone in the Pledge of Allegiance, and then Barbara began to speak, rallying the crowd as she argued that they shouldn't accept the conditions of their school. She announced the plan: they would refuse to attend school until they got what they rightfully deserved. They would go on strike. Most students agreed, and many stayed after school to make signs and posters.

The student strike got the support of lawyers from the National Association for the Advancement of Colored People (the NAACP), who were impressed with how well-organized they were. Though the school board mostly ignored the student demands, the lawyers did not. They filed a federal lawsuit, and three years later it was one of the five cases that became part of the landmark Supreme Court decision *Brown vs. Board of Education of Topeka*. Though Barbara's story isn't as well known as those of Rosa Parks or Dr. Martin Luther King Jr., there are many who say that her nonviolent student-led protest helped start the civil rights movement.

RADICAL MONARCHS

FOUNDED IN OAKLAND, CALIFORNIA, 2014

THEY MAY EARN BADGES, but when these girls march through the streets they're not selling cookies—they're leading protests. And if you look closely, you'll see that these aren't your average badges. Coding? Healing? Entrepreneurship? You got it. These are the Radical Monarchs, a social justice troop for young girls of color who want to learn about community, history, self-love, and activism.

The Radical Monarchs started when Lupita, a fourth grader, wanted to join a Girl Scouts troop. Her mom thought it was a great idea but was concerned that Lupita, who is Mexican-American, would be the only girl of color in the troop. Lupita's mom asked herself: *What would it look like to create a social justice troop that focused on girls of color?* She casually mentioned the idea to Lupita—and the budding activist would not let it go, begging her mom to get it started.

> "We are still kids, but that doesn't mean we are not powerful."
> —Luna, age ten

Lupita and her mom reached out to classmates and friends, and soon Troop 1 was born, with twelve girls between the ages of nine and eleven, and two grown-up troop leaders. The curriculum is shaped by what the girls want to learn. They've camped, hiked, gardened, and visited a Native American sweat lodge. They combine activism and current events with useful, empowering skills. When all the girls got excited about learning how to code, the troop leaders designed a whole unit around it. The Monarchs got to learn the basics of this crucial computer skill, and they even designed and built their own original projects: social justice emojis and an app that lets you take a selfie with a *"herstorical"* role model. A unit on Radical Entrepreneurship enabled the girls to identify the kinds of products they'd like to make (and sell!), and soon they were making their own body oils and earrings. And a unit on Radical Beauty focused on developing positive body image and self-esteem—messages the girls are actively sharing back at school.

The Monarchs also focus on *doing*—when issues arise in their communities, they discuss them. Many of the girls were upset after the 2016 presidential election, so they talked it out, asking each other: What do you want to *do?* The girls decided they wanted to march and to speak up on behalf of their city and community. So the Radical Monarchs joined sixty thousand other concerned citizens at the Women's March in Oakland, California, on January 21, 2017. Several weeks later they spoke at a city council meeting, where they advocated for Oakland to become a sanctuary city that protects and stands up for all of its residents—even those who might not have the same citizenship status.

Of course, they have also faced criticism: some people think it's inappropriate for girls to learn about complicated political and protest histories. Others think they shouldn't be taught to march in the streets or hold Black Lives Matter signs. But the Monarchs will tell you that they're *already* aware of injustice. They see it every day in their neighborhoods and schools and in government. They're developing the tools to navigate the world with confidence and to work to make it better. And to those who say they're being brainwashed? "Girls get brainwashed by the media every day," they reply. "The Radical Monarchs are *undoing* the brainwashing."

MEGAN GREENWELL AND ILIANA MONTAUK

PUBLISHED IN BERKELEY, CALIFORNIA, 1999

In November of 1999, Megan Greenwell and Iliana Montauk gathered for a staff meeting of *The Jacket*, the school newspaper of Berkeley High School, to brainstorm article ideas. An advisor mentioned a local news story: a seventeen-year-old girl named Chanti had died of carbon monoxide poisoning in a nearby apartment building, and her fifteen-year-old sister was found unconscious. They had both been discovered by their eighteen-year-old roommate.

As the student reporters discussed the story, they noticed odd details that none of the local news coverage had mentioned: the apartment was just blocks from Berkeley High, but the girls weren't enrolled there. Two of them had recently come to the United States from India, and all three girls worked at a local Indian restaurant. Why were these young people working and not attending Berkeley High? Were they enrolled in any school at all? Iliana, an editor, assigned fifteen-year-old Megan to investigate this angle.

Through her initial research, Megan learned that the girls lived in an apartment separate from their parents—and the landlord of both apartment buildings was the owner of the restaurant where the girls worked. She also discovered that this landlord was present when Chanti was found, and that he had taken care of her funeral arrangements. Who was this man, and why was he connected to Chanti in so many different ways? Megan was surprised that the local news was not making any of these connections.

Megan and Iliana reached out to a teacher who connected them to members of the local South Asian immigrant community. Once Megan and Iliana gained the trust of these sources, they learned that the landlord was known to bring poor young women over from India to work in his restaurants. The girls weren't paid, and they weren't allowed to go to school. It was a form of modern indentured servitude—and it's illegal. The students wondered: Had Chanti been a servant? Could her death have been prevented?

Suddenly, the two teens were working on a very serious story. They were intimidated by what they'd uncovered, but they knew they had to keep going. After consulting with school officials and a lawyer, Megan and Iliana published their article, "Young Indian Immigrant Dies in Berkeley Apartment, South Asian Community Says 'Indentured Servitude' May Be to Blame." Soon after, the Berkeley police reopened their investigation—and uncovered an enormous human smuggling operation, as well as reports of abuse. The landlord was arrested, convicted, and sentenced to eight years in prison. The case led to the creation of stricter human trafficking laws in California, and journalists from all over the world flocked to Berkeley to cover the story—and to interview the two young women who cracked the case wide open.

CELESTE TINAJERO

Water leaked from old faucets. Crumpled paper towels littered the floor. Toilets clogged and overflowed, spilling precious water. That's what Celeste Tinajero saw every time she went into the bathrooms at her high school in Reno, Nevada. Wasted water, paper, and energy—Celeste couldn't stand it. And her fellow Eco Warriors felt the same way.

> **"I am inspired by the chain reaction of change."**

The Eco Warriors is an environmental club started by Celeste's brother, Hector. After Celeste joined, the group decided to tackle the waste they were seeing on campus. They did research and learned that their school's facilities hadn't been updated since the buildings were constructed four decades before. Celeste applied for a grant from a coalition of environmental organizations in Reno, and she received first place. Reed High School was awarded $12,000 to update its bathroom facilities. The school was able to install low-flush toilets, automatic hand dryers, and new auto-sensor lighting and faucets that couldn't be left on. These upgrades saved water, paper, and energy—and also saved the school a lot of money.

But why stop there? The bathrooms weren't the only waste issue that Celeste saw on campus. Buoyed by the club's success, Celeste applied for another grant. This one addressed the problem of single-use plastic water bottles. Hundreds of students used them, and almost all of the bottles ended up in the trash. This is reflective of a broader trend: Americans alone use fifty million single-use plastic bottles per year, but only about 23 percent are recycled. The rest end up in landfills—or in the ocean. The average American uses more than 150 disposable bottles a year!

Once again, Celeste's grant proposal was selected, and this time her school received $3,500 to install "hydration stations" where students could fill reusable water bottles. Celeste and the Eco Warriors also lobbied the school to stop selling bottled water, and they worked hard to spread the word about the new stations. They made sure that students understood the global impact of their daily choices and got excited about reducing waste on campus. It worked: students loved the refillable water stations, and in one year they saved thirty-seven thousand plastic water bottles from being used!

Celeste's commitment to preserving the planet led her to make strong connections with local environmental organizations, and after she graduated, she went on to work on a campaign to ban plastic bags in the city of Reno. She has won many awards for her activism and advocacy, and she is passionate about speaking to other young people about what they can do to make a difference.

CONSTANCE MCMILLAN

BORN IN FULTON, MISSISSIPPI, 1992

Constance McMillan grew up in a small conservative town. When she was in fifth grade, she realized she was gay. She didn't tell anyone until eighth grade, when she came out as bisexual. By the time she was a high school senior in 2010, Constance identified as a lesbian and had her first girlfriend. They wanted to do what lots of other high school couples do: get dressed up, go to prom, and dance the night away.

There had never been an openly gay couple at her high school before, so Constance asked her principal if they were allowed to attend prom. The principal said no. They would be allowed to attend the prom *separately*, he said. But if they danced together, or held hands, or anything like that, they would be kicked out.

Constance thought this was ridiculous ("I'm not going to go to prom and pretend I'm not gay," she said), but at first she accepted it. She didn't know there was anything she *could* do about it. A few weeks later she asked her principal another question: could she wear a tuxedo to the prom? Constance had never liked wearing dresses or girly clothes, and she thought a tux would be cool to wear. Once again, the principal said no: "Boys wear tuxedos, girls wear dresses."

By this point, Constance was fed up. This wasn't just an unfair school rule. This felt like discrimination. She contacted the local chapter of the American Civil Liberties Union (ACLU) and told them what was happening. The ACLU sent a letter to her school, letting them know that they were violating her rights by blocking her

from bringing her girlfriend to prom. The school's response? They cancelled the prom. Not just for Constance and her girlfriend—for everyone.

> **"Stand up like I did. It was hard, but it was worth it."**

By this time, the story of the teenage girl who wanted to bring her girlfriend to prom had spread, and Constance's story was making headlines. She received support from people all over the country—except from her hometown. Many of her classmates blamed her for the cancelled prom, and some people in town thought Constance should've just kept her mouth shut. This was hard for Constance, who was relatively shy and had never seen herself as an activist. But she knew who she was, and she wasn't going to be mistreated.

Constance sued her school district, and she won. The judge ruled that the school had violated Constance's First Amendment rights. Constance received a large sum of money, but something even better came out of the lawsuit: the school agreed to a new nondiscrimination policy that included sexual orientation. Constance never got to go to her prom, but by standing up for her rights she ensured that future gay and lesbian students at her school would be able to.

CORDELIA LONGO

One day at school, eighth grader Cordelia Longo experienced a problem that a lot of women are familiar with: she got her period and needed supplies. She went from bathroom to bathroom, but all of the outdated tampon and pad vending machines were either empty or broken (and they took her last few dimes). She was frustrated and embarrassed—and also pretty mad. It didn't seem fair that schools provided toilet paper and paper towels for all students but that girls had to buy menstrual supplies (if there were any). It's not like menstruation was their choice. It is a natural bodily function that almost all young women experience monthly. She talked to some of her friends afterward and realized almost all of them had similar stories of anxiously trying to find supplies at school, only to find empty or broken machines.

So Cordelia started a petition asking the school to update its menstrual product machines and to provide free tampons and pads. She quickly gathered more than a hundred signatures, and they weren't just from other girls. Many supportive boys and teachers signed on, too. In addition to the petition, Cordelia wrote a letter to the administration arguing that by not providing free menstrual products the school was penalizing girls for a bodily function they could not choose or opt out of.

Cordelia's action was inspired by two things. She had recently taken a social justice class at school, where she'd learned about activism, equality, and how to work for change. She was also deeply motivated by the 2016 election and the way that Hillary Clinton ran her campaign. Cordelia admired Hillary's strength and courage in the face of so much negativity. She watched when Hillary won the popular vote but lost the Electoral College vote, and Hillary's resilience made Cordelia want to work hard for gender equality.

"This seemed like something I should fix."

While the school was reviewing the petition and letter, Cordelia took matters into her own hands. She knew that girls' cycles wouldn't wait for the principal to make a decision. Cordelia used her own allowance money to purchase baskets, tampons, and pads, and she placed them in each of the school's girls' bathrooms. The final touch? She added a little note on each basket with a quote from Hillary: "Women's rights are human rights. Human rights are women's rights."

The school administration was impressed by Cordelia's efforts. "It's so great for a fourteen-year-old girl to say, 'This is wrong and we should not pay for this,'" said the vice principal. Within a week, the school had restocked the machines and disabled the coin operation, making the supplies totally free. Cordelia's efforts made such an impact that the local high school did the same thing!

MEMORY BANDA

BORN IN CHIRADZULU, MALAWI, 1996

I'LL MARRY WHEN I WANT

I'll marry when I want
My mother can't force me to marry
My father cannot force me to marry
My uncle my aunt my brother or sister
Cannot force me to marry
No one in the world can force me to marry
I'll marry when I want
Even if you beat me, even if you chase me away
Even if you do anything bad to me
I'll marry when I want
But not before I am well-educated
and not before I am all grown-up
I'll marry when I want.

THIS POEM WAS WRITTEN by Eileen Piri, a thirteen-year-old girl from a village in the east African country of Malawi, a nation where child marriage has long been a traditional practice. The poem became widely known after a young activist named Memory Banda read it during a speech in 2015. Memory described the poem as "a warrior's cry," and she went on to tell the audience about her own journey as an activist and leader in the fight against child marriage. Memory's speech has been viewed online over two million times.

> "You will never know you are a leader until you stand up."

Memory is an example of someone who has made big changes in the world but started small, on the local level. Memory wasn't a child bride, but her younger sister was. Memory had long watched the suffering of other girls in her village who'd been married off quite young. She saw them stop going to school, endure abuse from violent, much older husbands, and often become sick or even die of complications from childbirth. At thirteen, Memory knew that wasn't the life she wanted for herself. When her younger sister started being prepared for marriage, Memory decided to take a powerful stand.

She didn't begin by trying to end child marriage—instead, she tried to empower the girls who were already married. Memory realized that she wasn't the only young woman to have big dreams for her future, and she wanted to encourage the young brides to not give up on their dreams just because they were married. Since most girls who married stopped going to school, Memory thought it would be a good idea to offer them literacy classes.

She put up flyers in her town and met regularly with the girls who showed up. It wasn't just Memory teaching the girls—she learned a lot from them, too. Memory encouraged the girls to tell their personal stories and to share the challenges they faced. Many of the girls opened up about being abused and how they felt trapped because they were financially dependent on their new husbands. Most of the girls had dropped out of school, and some even became infected with HIV. In this space, where the girls could share personal stories, they were able to form powerful connections and see how their experiences weren't just isolated incidents but part of a larger, dangerous pattern. It was clear that girls were not valued in their community.

Memory wanted to change this, so she decided to go to the community leaders. This was not easy. The leaders are very powerful figures who demand great respect. It was not at all normal for a woman to speak to them, let alone a young girl demanding change. But Memory wasn't alone; she was working closely with the girls from her literacy group, as well as two international organizations that help support young female leaders.

With their help, Memory put together a collection of the girls' stories to present to the leaders. The first time Memory spoke to them, she was terribly nervous. She felt small and scared, but she knew that her message was important. She shared the brides' stories of abuse and fear, and she asked the leaders to consider changing the laws and ending the hurtful traditions. She told them: the girls want education. They want the chance to pursue their dreams.

> "I've always been that kind of person pushing for what I believe in. It's very important that women and girls all over the world believe in themselves and push for what they believe in. Even if it doesn't work out, at least you can say that you tried."

The reactions were not very positive. Most of the leaders dismissed Memory and the other girls and didn't take them seriously. They figured Memory and the girls would give up and go away. Many of the women in the community were critical: they called Memory "stupid" and "stubborn"; they said she was being disrespectful of the cultural traditions. Memory disagreed. If a tradition is harmful, why should it continue? And why shouldn't she be the one to speak up?

Memory and the girls kept pushing, despite the criticism. They returned to the leaders again and again and kept speaking up. They connected with female leaders in other parts of the country and presented to more than sixty village chiefs, and even to members of Parliament. Little by little, Memory was able to

gain the respect of these elders. By sharing the girls' stories, she helped create understanding. By being persistent and refusing to back down, she showed that she should be taken seriously. Eventually, in 2013, the traditional leaders decided to change their laws; they declared that no girl under age eighteen could be forced to marry.

That was just the start. Memory had helped change local laws, but the goal was to change the entire country. A large network of women and men kept working to change child marriage laws in Malawi. Memory began giving speeches all over the world, spreading the message about the dangers of child marriage and the importance of supporting girls and young women. Her powerful voice brought attention to the issue. Finally, in 2015, Malawi passed a law that raised the legal age for marriage from fifteen to eighteen. And in 2017, Malawi amended its constitution for good. Life for young girls in Malawi is not perfect, but these laws, and the many people Memory works with, have brought about great improvements.

And yet Memory is not done. She knows that girls all over the world face challenges, especially when it comes to education. She is an advocate not just for girls from Malawi, or from Africa, but for girls everywhere. She speaks and presents in cities and countries across the globe, bringing a message of girl empowerment everywhere she goes.

RADEN ADJENG KARTINI

Raden Adjeng Kartini (known as "Kartini") was born into an aristocratic family in Indonesia (but was then a Dutch colony called Java). Kartini was especially close with her three younger sisters. Their father supported education for his daughters and Kartini and her sisters attended a Dutch school. But when each turned twelve, they were forced to leave school and go into seclusion at home until a marriage was arranged. This traditional practice, called *pingitan*, was common for upper-class Indonesian girls.

> "Even though I shall not be happy after I have reached my goal, though I may give way before it is half reached, I shall die gladly, for the path will then have been broken, and I shall have helped to clear the way which leads to freedom and independence for the native women."

While Kartini had a deep love for her country and culture, leaving school and waiting around for marriage was *not* okay with her. Kartini was a brilliant student who'd learned to read and write in Dutch, which was very unusual for an Indonesian girl at the time. She'd had a taste of what a life of education, ideas, and freedom could be like—yet tradition said that she would be forced to marry someone she'd never met, who might already have another wife or two.

Kartini went into seclusion, but she refused to be denied an education. She decided to teach herself. She spent all her time reading, studying, and writing hundreds of letters to a number of prominent Dutch feminists and writers, who eagerly corresponded with her. They exchanged ideas and support, and Kartini explored and expressed her views on everything from colonialism to marriage.

Kartini's sisters soon joined her in seclusion. Over the next four years they formed a deep bond, becoming committed to women's independence and education and planning to open a school together. Though cut off from society, they managed to learn about the world through books, magazines, newspapers, letters, and each other.

Kartini's seclusion ended when she finally agreed to be married at age nineteen. Yet she still fulfilled her dream of starting a school for girls; it opened in 1904 with 120 students. Sadly, Kartini died soon after the school opened, but her impact was just beginning. Her sisters carried on her legacy, and the letters she had written as a teenager were turned into a hugely popular book that was translated into many languages. Her ideas about women's rights shaped the Indonesian women's movement as well as the country's independence movement. Several schools have been founded in Kartini's name, and in 1964, the president of Indonesia declared Kartini's birthday "Kartini's Day." It is one of Indonesia's biggest national holidays, and schoolgirls across the country dress up and pay tribute to their heroine.

S. E. HINTON

BORN IN TULSA, OKLAHOMA, 1968

SUSAN ELOISE HINTON may have received a D in her high school creative writing class, but she also got a book deal on the same day that she got her diploma. She wrote her first novel, *The Outsiders*, when she was sixteen years old, and it remains one of the best-selling young-adult novels of all time. Maybe she got the D because she was too busy writing her own book at home!

Susan grew up in a rough neighborhood. Her family didn't have much money, and her deeply religious mother was cruel and abusive. Susan was considered a tomboy; she wore jeans (not skirts), hung out with mostly boys, and liked to ride horses, go duck hunting, and play football. She also loved to read and write. Reading was a way for Susan to escape from the problems she faced at home, and she devoured every book she could get her hands on. Writing stories helped her process her feelings, but her mother didn't approve and would get angry when she caught Susan writing. Once, she took some of the stories that Susan was working on and threw them in the trash. But Susan was able to rescue them; she disobeyed her mother and kept on writing.

As she got older, Susan felt unsatisfied by the books that were aimed at teenagers. They all seemed to tell happy stories about perfect teenage girls named Mary Jane who go to the prom with the star football player. In other words, the books didn't reflect her life at all. Most of the guys she hung out with were considered "greasers" or "hoods"—in other words, they were "bad kids" from struggling families. People had all kinds of judgments about these guys, but to Susan they were her friends. They were individuals with real lives

and real feelings who often suffered bullying and abuse, mainly from the rich kids in town whose parents worked in the booming oil business—the "soc" kids (pronounced "sohsh," as in "social").

Life got even tougher when Susan was fifteen. Her dad was diagnosed with cancer, which made an already difficult home life even worse. Susan was also increasingly aware of the social tensions in town. After her good friend got beaten up by a soc on his way home from seeing a movie, she was furious. She was sick of seeing her friends treated like that, just because of where they were growing up, how they dressed, and how much money their parents did (or didn't) have.

She sat down to write about it, and the story just started pouring out. She had no plan or plot at first—she was just writing to help herself work through her feelings, as she had done for so long.

But it was more than just an angry rant. She soon realized that she had enough ideas and characters to make a whole book. It was her chance to write a story that accurately reflected her life and the lives of her outcast friends.

Over the next year and a half, she wrote four complete drafts of a novel. She wrote before, after, and sometimes even during school. She called the book *The Outsiders*; it told the gritty, often violent story of a group of young greaser boys who clashed with the soc boys (and who liked some of the soc girls). The characters have memorable names, like Ponyboy, Two-Bit, Dallas, Sodapop, and Cherry Valance, and they also have complex emotions and individual struggles. Though the book was fiction, it was based on what Susan saw at school, at home, and in town. The opening scene of the book describes how Ponyboy was jumped on his way home from seeing a movie. The dialogue was based on how Susan's friends actually talked, swear words and all.

The hardest part about writing *The Outsiders* was knowing when to stop, because Susan had so much to say. When she finally finished it, she was a junior in high school. She was proud of the story, but she never imagined its being published. She showed it to her friend's mom, who was a children's book writer. The woman was so impressed that she showed it to a literary agent in New York City. He was also impressed—for so many years, books for teenagers had been written by adults trying to remember what it was like to be a teenager. And here was an intense, emotionally charged novel written *for* teenagers *by* a teenager. He knew it was going to be a hit, and on the day she received her diploma at her high school graduation, Susan Hinton also got a book deal.

But there was one problem: the publisher didn't think anyone would believe that Susan had written it. It was all about boys, and there was violence and drinking and smoking and swearing. A teenage girl as the writer? No way! So they suggested she use her initials and publish as "S. E. Hinton." Susan agreed, and for

many years people assumed (and many still do) that the author of *The Outsiders* was a man.

The Outsiders was published while Susan was a freshman in college. It was an instant success, and people went wild for this intense new book by a seventeen-year-old author. It was all very exciting, but also intimidating. People immediately wanted to know what Susan would write next, and she felt the pressure. She felt stuck—and began to worry that she was out of good ideas. A good friend encouraged her, and she committed to writing two new pages every day. It took her three years, but by the time she graduated from college she'd completed her next novel, *That Was Then, This Is Now*. She followed with more young-adult novels featuring struggling young male protagonists, like *Rumble Fish* and *Tex*.

Several of her books were made into movies, and forty years after it was published, *The Outsiders* remains one of the best-selling young-adult novels of all time. It's credited with changing the way that young adult fiction is written—and how teenagers read. It has sold more than fourteen million copies and is taught in many schools—including Susan's alma mater, Will Rogers High School in Tulsa, where it all began.

MARY SHELLEY

It began as a dare during a boring summer vacation in the year 1816. Eighteen-year-old Mary Godwin, her then-boyfriend (and future husband), the poet Percy Bysshe Shelley, and several others had joined the poet Lord Byron at a lake house in Geneva, Switzerland. The plan had been to spend the days outdoors, boating and hiking, but terrible weather kept them cooped up inside. They stayed up late into the night, discussing literature by candlelight, while thunderstorms raged outside. It was the perfect setting for reading ghost stories out loud, which they did one evening. Afterward, Lord Byron issued a challenge to his fellow writers: "We will each write a ghost story."

For the next several days, Mary tried to think of a good idea, but she couldn't. She felt frustrated, because she really wanted to write a great ghost story. Then, one night, inspiration struck in the form of a nightmare. In the dream, she saw terrifying, vivid images of a man kneeling beside a dead body . . . but the body was coming back to life. The body rose from its grave and opened its yellow eyes and—Mary woke up!

The dream was so vivid, she had to capture it on paper. She began to write her ghost story immediately. The others grew tired of the ghost story challenge and quit, but Mary kept at it, drawing more inspiration from the bleak landscape that surrounded them, the gloomy weather, and her own experiences with loss and sadness. Mary's mother, the famous early-feminist writer Mary Wollstonecraft, had died soon after giving birth to Mary. And Mary had run away from her father to be with Percy Shelley, and at seventeen had given birth to a daughter who did not survive.

Mary finished the story that summer and decided to expand it into a novel. She worked on it for the next year, and *Frankenstein* was published anonymously when Mary Shelley was just twenty years old. It told the frightening tale of Victor Frankenstein, a young scientist who creates a monster by reanimating a corpse. Percy Shelley wrote the introduction, and many people assumed that he was also the author, as no one could believe that a woman could write such a dark, gruesome novel. Four years later another edition came out, this time crediting Mary Shelley as the author.

Frankenstein was republished several more times during Mary's life, and it has never gone out of print. It has come to be recognized as the first work of science fiction, and to this day many people don't realize that the most famous monster of all time came from the imagination (and nightmares) of a teenage girl.

HABEN GIRMA

HABEN GIRMA CAN hear some sounds at very high frequencies, and she can perceive movement and some colors, but she is legally blind and deaf. Deafblindness occurs on a spectrum, meaning that deafblind people can have a range of hearing and vision capabilities. Haben is able to speak clearly and also communicates using technology (a digital braille device enables her to immediately read what someone types onto a separate wireless keyboard). As a child, Haben was able to attend public schools that had well-trained special-education teachers who could support her. This is something her mother did *not* take for granted: it was why she had come to America in the first place.

Before Haben was born, her mother had fled war-torn Eritrea, a small country in eastern Africa. She walked for two weeks, traveling at night and hiding in the jungle during the day, until she reached the country of Sudan. After several months there, a refugee organization helped her come to America. In California, Haben's mother met her father, an Eritrean who'd grown up in Ethiopia.

In elementary and middle school, Haben attended mainstream classes with nondisabled students. The public schools in Oakland, California, had teachers for the blind who helped convert print materials to braille. Haben would leave her mainstream classes for one hour each day to learn braille, cane travel, and other blindness skills. She loved books (especially Nancy Drew mysteries) and learning, but always wished she could make more friends at school.

During her sophomore year of high school, Haben set her mind on a new challenge. It involved getting on an airplane with a group of students and teachers and flying all the way to Mali to a small African village in need of a school. Haben wanted to join the organization that took students to do this service project. And this freaked her parents out.

> "The danger of a single disability story is that the public expects people to conform to that story. My story is one more story from which the public can learn. We all deserve the opportunity to develop our own unique talents and interests."

Her parents asked, "Why don't you volunteer here in Oakland instead?" Haben explained that she did in fact volunteer in Oakland—and now she wanted to volunteer in Mali, too. Her parents asked, "Can't you build a school somewhere closer to home?" Haben insisted that she wanted to build *this* specific school. Then her parents asked, "But how can you build a school?" Every time she heard a question like that, Haben became even more convinced that she wanted to go. She wanted to show everyone—including herself—that she could travel and make an impact. That she could do *anything.* She pointed out that everyone on the trip would be facing challenges, not just her. Even though the other students could hear, she reasoned, they wouldn't understand the local language. Even though they could see, they'd never built a school before. To Haben, they were all on the same level and could all learn together.

Haben persisted, eventually convincing her parents to let her go. At age fifteen, Haben traveled halfway across the world to Mali and joined other students in building a school. She learned to sift sand and make bricks. The trip was not without its challenges, but that was exactly why Haben had wanted to go: to prove that she could meet challenges and navigate them on her own. The people in the village had never met a deafblind person before, so they got to encounter something new as well.

> "I needed to prove to myself that I *can* make a difference. I needed to experience making an impact, and I did."

The trip showed Haben and her parents that she could be independent, which was very helpful when it came time for her to apply for college. Haben opted for a school in another state, and while her parents had hoped she'd go somewhere close by, they knew now that she would be fine living far from home. During the summer between high school and college she went to a blindness training program, where she and other blind adults learned independent life skills that most able-bodied people might not even think twice about. They learned nonvisual techniques for everything from firing up a radial arm saw to baking banana cream pie to crossing streets. Haben already had some of these skills, but she wanted to learn as many as possible before going off on her own.

Once she arrived at college, Haben was very happy. She was thrilled to be there, and she loved her classes. But one thing kept bothering her: every day she went to the dining hall to eat but was not able to read the menu because it wasn't available in braille. She ended up eating whatever the cafeteria workers put on her tray. She asked the cafeteria manager to provide the menu in an accessible format, and he told her he was too busy.

That wasn't fair, but what could she do? If she complained, would people laugh at her? She'd grown up hearing stories about suffering back in Eritrea, and here she was in America, at a top college, complaining about not having a menu? But the more she thought about it, Haben realized it wasn't just about a menu—it was about *access*. Equal access. She was probably not the only student with a disability to be facing some kind of challenge on a college campus. It was not just about her problem with the dining hall: it was a much bigger issue.

She spoke up again and informed the cafeteria manager that the Americans with Disabilities Act (ADA) prohibits discrimination against people with disabilities. Haben told him that if he didn't start providing access, she would sue. And what happened? The manager suddenly had time to email the menu to Haben (which she read in braille, thanks to a special device) so she could make food choices just like everyone else. Haben got the menu every day, and the next year, when a blind student arrived on campus, that student got the menus emailed to him, too.

As a lifelong volunteer, Haben was committed to helping others, and these experiences led her to realize her calling: she wanted to become a lawyer and help enforce civil-rights laws. She went on to become the first deafblind person to graduate from Harvard Law School, where she also performed with the ballroom dance team. She is now a lawyer, author, and public speaker who travels the world teaching organizations about the importance of designing accessible programs and services for everyone.

HELEN KELLER AND LAURA BRIDGMAN

Helen Keller was born with the ability to see and hear, but an illness before age two left her deaf and blind. By age seven, she'd developed about sixty signs on her own, which she used to communicate with her parents and siblings. She could feel the beat of music, which she enjoyed, and could identify family members by the vibration of their footsteps. Her major breakthrough came when her family hired a teacher, Anne Sullivan, to work with her. Anne had also lost her vision as a child and had just graduated from a special school for the blind. Anne and Helen grew very close, and Anne successfully taught Helen to communicate. Anne and Helen spent the next fifty years together, and Helen went on to be the first deaf person in America to get a college degree. She taught herself to speak and could read people's lips with her hands. Helen became known worldwide as a powerful speaker who advocated for peace and justice.

Fifty years before Helen Keller, there had been another deafblind girl who became well known in the United States. Her name was Laura Bridgman, and she was the first deafblind person to receive an education in America. Like Helen, Laura had also become sick as a baby: she'd had scarlet fever, which caused her to lose her sight, her hearing, and her sense of taste. To communicate, she developed a very basic form of sign language. Despite these signs, Laura was ignored by most of her family and often had violent outbursts and tantrums. No one knew what to do with Laura.

In 1837, at the age of eight, she was sent to the newly opened Perkins School for the Blind. No one there had taught a deafblind person to communicate, but eager teachers developed innovative methods to teach Laura various forms of tactile signing. Soon Laura could write her name, read braille, and do math equations. Laura became something of a celebrity after the British writer Charles Dickens wrote about her during a visit to America. Crowds of people began to visit the school on Saturdays, when it was open to the public, just to watch Laura read braille or point out locations on a map. She remained at Perkins for her entire adult life, helping teach younger students, including a young Anne Sullivan, who learned from Laura before she was hired to teach Helen Keller.

When Anne left Perkins to live with the Keller family, she brought with her a doll wearing a dress that Laura had sewn. A few years later, in 1888, Anne returned to Perkins. She introduced eight-year-old Helen to Laura—the only time that these two notable deafblind women ever met.

PHIONA MUTESI

PHIONA MUTESI GREW UP in the Katwe slum, one of the poorest neighborhoods of Kampala, the capital of the east African country of Uganda. It was a dangerous place, with no sewage system, very little food, and garbage-filled streets. Phiona couldn't read or write because she had to drop out of school at age six to help her mother sell corn in the streets. Sometimes, after a long day of hard work, she would be robbed of the money she'd earned and return home empty-handed.

One day when she was nine, she followed her older brother through the streets, hoping he would lead her to some food. Phiona watched in secret as her brother joined a group of children and one adult man crowded in silence around a black-and-white checkered board. They took turns carefully moving tiny statues across the board. Phiona was enthralled: the game was beautiful, and she was amazed by how happy her brother and the others looked as they played. The game was chess, and Phiona immediately wanted to understand it.

The man who was teaching the game finally spotted her and invited her to join them. His name was Robert, and he'd grown up in Katwe. He had come back to help young people by teaching them to play chess.

Chess is a game of skill, strategy, and determination. It's about overcoming challenges and beating your opponent by making smart choices. In this way, Robert reasoned, the children of Katwe could relate. And he was right. Phiona began coming to play chess every day, walking several miles each way. Robert provided food for the chess players, as well as coaching.

Phiona lost her first fifty matches or so because she was too eager to beat her opponent right away. Despite this, Robert could tell that she had a gift. Over time, Phiona learned how to calm down and be a wise, patient player, and soon the young girl was outsmarting her coach. Chess was the one thing in her life that Phiona could control. She became focused and incredibly skilled, and two years after she first saw a chessboard, Phiona was the Girls Chess Champion of Uganda.

In 2011, Phiona and several boys from Katwe represented Uganda in the International Children's Chess Tournament in the Sudan. It was Phiona's first time leaving her country, which meant it was also her first time on an airplane, in a hotel, and using a toilet and shower. She felt like a queen.

Phiona and the Katwe team competed against players from sixteen other African nations, many of whom came from wealthy cities and had trained in elite private schools and universities. The Katwe team shocked everyone when they won the championship and brought a giant trophy home. They were greeted as heroes.

In the following years, Phiona traveled all over the world to compete against players of all ages from many countries. She was often one of the youngest players there, and her playing was impressive. She went on to earn the title of Woman Candidate Master, the first step toward being a Grandmaster (the highest title that a chess player can achieve).

Phiona's story became widely known in 2016, when a movie about her life was released by Disney. *The Queen of Katwe* is based on a nonfiction book by a journalist, and with the money from the book and film, Phiona was able to move her family out of the Katwe slum and into a nice house on a fertile plot of land.

PRINCESS PING YANG

BORN IN ANCIENT CHINA, 598 CE

Princess Ping Yang was the daughter of Li Yuan, a military general who became the founder of ancient China's Tang dynasty—thanks in great part to Ping Yang's assistance.

When Ping Yang was seventeen, her dad, who'd risen from peasant life to a position of power, began plotting to overthrow the cruel, greedy emperor. Before Li Yuan attacked, he warned Ping Yang and her husband, who was a palace guard, because he didn't want them to be harmed. When Ping Yang and her husband got the message, her husband was worried that it might be dangerous for them to escape together. Ping Yang told him to go, arguing that as a woman, she'd be able to hide

more easily if she was alone. Her husband agreed, and suddenly Ping Yang was on her own.

She left the palace in the dark of night and made her way across the Yellow River. She returned to her hometown and her family's estate. In the village, she found the local people suffering from starvation due to drought and the tyranny of the corrupt emperor. She immediately opened up her family's grain supply and began to feed everyone. The people were grateful, and when she told them she was building an army, they agreed to join her. Then she sold her family's home and most of their land and used the money to buy supplies, including horses, food, and weapons.

She worked to convince others to join her, and soon she had several hundred men willing to follow her. Some were rebel leaders, and many were peasants. They roamed from village to village, but instead of allowing them to loot and pillage, Ping Yang made rules that her men had to follow: they would not harm people but would instead give them food and water. This kindness would win the villagers' loyalty and trust *without* any need to resort to violence.

Ping Yang's methods worked, and within a few months the seventeen-year-old was in command of an army of seventy thousand men, known as "the Army of the Lady." The emperor's troops found out about them and began to attack. The Army of the Lady stayed strong, and soon they joined forces with Ping Yang's father and his troops—and Ping Yang's husband, who had joined her father in the fight against the emperor. Together, they stormed the palace and created a new dynasty. Ping Yang was made a princess in honor of her great achievements.

KHUTULUN

Khutulun—her name means "moonlight"—was the niece of the feared ruler of the Mongol Empire, Kublai Khan, and the great-great-granddaughter of the legendary warrior Genghis Khan. She had fourteen older brothers, and she grew up learning to fight and wrestle. Wrestling was an important part of Mongolian culture, along with horseback riding and archery. Khutulun, it turned out, excelled at all three. Like many women of the Mongol Empire, she was big, strong, and powerful.

As a young teenager, Khutulun joined many public wrestling competitions and gained a reputation as the woman no man could beat. The prize for winning wrestling matches was horses, and Khutulun's impressive herd grew to include thousands of these valuable and prized animals. Khutulun often rode alongside her father across the steppes of Mongolia as they defended their territory. The explorer Marco Polo met Khutulun and described her amazing battle technique: she would "make a dash at the host of the enemy and seize some man thereout, as deftly as a hawk pounces on a bird, and carry him to her father; and this she did many a time."

Soon the teenage Khutulun was seen as a highly desirable wife. She had royal blood and connections to major military figures, and she was a fearless warrior herself. Her parents were desperate for her to marry, as it was unheard of for a woman not to be married by the time she was twenty. But there was a problem: Khutulun refused to marry anyone who was physically inferior to her. To determine the strength of her

potential suitors, she insisted on wrestling each and every one. And she kept beating them all. She ordered that any man who lost had to give her a hundred horses. So that herd got even bigger—legend says she had more than ten thousand horses!

Eventually Khutulun's parents gave up and stopped insisting that she marry. Once the pressure was lifted, she did get married—but *she* chose the guy. Khutulun continued to be a warrior, offering political and military strategy to her father. When he died, she had the honor of guarding his tomb. She has been a popular figure in Eastern and Western folklore for centuries, and is thought to be the basis for a famous opera by Giacomo Puccini, *Turandot*.

JOAN OF ARC

BORN IN FRANCE, 1412

Joan of Arc was born to a poor peasant family in a region of eastern France that had suffered greatly from an ongoing conflict between France and England. From an early age Joan was very sensitive and religious. She was uneducated, and she spent her days on the farm, tending animals.

Joan experienced her first vision around age twelve or thirteen. She was standing in her father's garden when she clearly saw three saints before her—Saint Catherine, Saint Margaret, and Saint Michael. She heard the voice of God tell her that she was the one to drive out the English and restore the nation of France. When the vision ended, Joan cried because it was so real and beautiful, but she didn't tell anyone what had happened. The visions continued for the next several years.

When Joan was sixteen, she heard God tell her it was time to go to King Charles VII to tell him she was the savior of France. She convinced a local leader to help her get to the Royal Court. He gave Joan horses, a sword, and an armed escort. To protect herself as she rode through enemy territory, Joan chopped off her hair and disguised herself as a male soldier.

Joan informed King Charles that she was sent by God to fight for France. Charles worried that she might be a sorceress, so he ordered a team of men to test her. After three weeks of exams, they declared Joan to be an honest person and not an evil witch. Joan rode straight into battle in the city of Orleans. Even though she had no battle experience, Joan proved to be an excellent commander and strategist. Under her leadership, the French troops won the battle of Orleans. Next, Joan was able to fulfill the ultimate prophecy by bringing Charles to Reims Cathedral to be crowned king. She was seen as a divine hero.

Eventually Joan was captured by the English, who charged her with witchcraft, heresy, and dressing like a man. She calmly maintained her innocence during the trial, despite violent threats. Nonetheless, the court sentenced her to death. At nineteen, Joan of Arc was publicly burned at the stake. Several years later, King Charles declared Joan innocent of all charges. She officially became a saint in 1920, and she is the patron saint of France.

ARTEMISIA GENTILESCHI

BORN IN ROME, ITALY, 1593

Artemisia Gentileschi was born into an artistic family at the end of the Renaissance period. Her father, Orazio, was a well-respected painter and a close friend of the famous painter Caravaggio. Artemisia's mother died when she was twelve, so she spent almost all of her time with her father. She didn't know how to read or write, but she loved to paint.

Because she was the daughter of a painter, she was able to become his apprentice, something that was generally off-limits to girls. Orazio soon realized how immensely talented his daughter was and encouraged her to keep painting. Artemisia debuted her first painting, *Susanna and the Elders*, at age seventeen. The painting depicted a classical biblical scene but was also very innovative in the way Artemisia composed the twisted body and expressive face of Susanna.

When she was eighteen, Artemisia was sexually assaulted by another painter, Agostino Tassi, who had hired her to be his daughter's art teacher. Artemisia reported the attack to her father, who was rightfully furious. Orazio petitioned the pope to hold a trial to convict Tassi, and a very public trial ensued. Artemisia bravely testified against her attacker and had to recall the assault in graphic detail. As was the custom in courts then, she also had to endure a medieval torture device called a thumbscrew that crushes the thumbs in order to get people to tell the truth. Despite the pain and public humiliation, Artemisia stuck by her story, and her attacker was convicted.

Soon after the trial, Artemisia painted what became one of her most famous paintings, *Judith Beheading Holofernes*. It shows the biblical figure of Judith cutting off the head of the invading general Holofernes. Many argue that Artemisia painted Judith to look just like her and used Tassi's face as the model for Holofernes. It is widely seen as a "revenge painting."

Although Tassi was convicted, Artemisia's reputation still suffered, so her father arranged a marriage for her and she moved to Florence, Italy. There she enjoyed great success, becoming the first woman accepted into the prestigious Academy of the Arts of Drawing. She befriended the nephew of Michelangelo, as well as the great scientist Galileo, and produced many more paintings.

As is the case with so many great female artists of the past, Artemisia faded into obscurity after her death. For centuries, art collectors and historians assumed that her paintings were done by her father. It wasn't until the twentieth century that people began to realize that she might be the artist, and as such, was one of the greatest post-Renaissance painters of all time.

YOU!

NAME

[Go ahead, fill it in. This is your page!]

BORN IN

town   state or country   year

NOW THAT YOU'VE READ about all kinds of rad young women, I hope you're feeling energized and motivated. Here's a reminder: *You are not any of the girls in this book*. Because you are *you*. You'll never be *just* like Misty Copeland or Tavi Gevinson or Amandla Stenberg—and they will never be just like you. That's the whole magnificent point of it all! You can take inspiration from them, but that's only *part* of it. You do the rest. *You* make your dreams come true.

Use this page to write or draw your story, and the next page to add your portrait. What makes you rad *right now*? What does your rad future look like? What are your goals and big dreams? And what will *you* do to make the world a better place?

Feeling inspired to make a difference, but wondering where to start?
Here are some suggestions for steps and actions that *anyone* can take.

TELL THE TRUTH ABOUT WHO YOU ARE AND WHAT YOU BELIEVE

This is definitely not easy—but it's always important. By telling our personal stories and truths, we can often help more people than just ourselves. And there are all kinds of ways to do this. Start a blog! Make a zine! Write an essay, a slam poem, a song! Or just open up to the people you're close to, and make sure your friends know who you really are.

MAKE A DIFFERENCE AT SCHOOL

If you aren't happy with something at your school, think about what you can do to make it better. Start a petition, write a letter, write an article for your school paper, or run for student government. Start a club and organize students around a particular cause or issue. Propose and organize an assembly on a topic you feel needs to be addressed. Invite a cool guest speaker. And if something major needs to happen, consider how you can effectively and safely take bigger action. Remember, if you want to do something that might get you in trouble or lead to controversy, make sure you're prepared for the consequences. Find a teacher, parent, or trusted adult advocate who has your back and can help you navigate challenging situations.

HAVE AN IMPACT ON LAWS AND LAWMAKERS

It's easy to feel like you can't make a difference when it comes to something as big and important as laws and politicians. But you never know until you try. Any person of any age can write a letter or email, make a phone call, or even pay a visit to their elected representatives. This includes your school board members, city council, the mayor, your state governor, congressional representatives, and even the president. These people were elected to represent you, even if you're too young to vote for them!

START YOUR OWN CLUB

There are lots of awesome organizations and groups you can join, but it's also fun to start your own. Think about what kind of club you'd like to have and what kinds of activities you'd like to do. Community service? Cool science experiments? Sports and outdoor activities? All you need is an idea and a purpose, a few committed friends, and a meeting place.

LEARN FROM YOUR PARENTS, TEACHERS, MENTORS, AND ELDERS

While this is a book about young people who have done amazing things, we have to acknowledge the importance of listening to and learning from the supportive adults in your life. When asked for advice on how to be rad, the first thing Lorella Praeli said was "Listen to your elders"—and she's right!

BE STRONG AND PLAY HARD

Playing sports is a great way to get exercise, use your body, make friends, and challenge yourself. To find the activity that's right for you, think about what you like to do and how you like to use your body. Do you want to be in the water, on a field, or high up on a climbing wall? Are you more of a team sports person, or do you prefer individual challenges? Do you want to try something calm, like yoga, or something more extreme, like roller derby? It's up to you! Remember: while many sports require special equipment and facilities, or expensive lessons and fees, there are lots of affordable ways to access fun activities. Check out local community centers, after-school programs, parks, and more. And remember: no matter what your gender, body type, or ability level is, *you can do it*! You'll never know until you try.

DO GREAT THINGS, EVEN IF PEOPLE DOUBT YOU

It can be really hard to believe in yourself when no one around seems to support you. But don't let that stop you! Most of the girls in this book were lucky enough to have supportive parents and teachers, but that's not always the case—and it doesn't mean you can't succeed. A number of the young people in these stories struggled with poverty and unreliable home lives, but each refused to let her circumstances limit her. They all found support in coaches, mentors, and friends who *did* believe in them, and they achieved greatness.

DO IT YOURSELF

Sometimes when we see successful people doing incredible things, we ask ourselves in disbelief, *How did she learn to do that?!* And sometimes we say to ourselves, *Well, I could never do that!* Whether it's recording an entire album, competing in the Olympics, or giving a speech in front of a huge audience, it's easy to think that *you* could never do that. It's true that some people are born with particular gifts and abilities, and some people have access and exposure to elite schools, training, and lessons. But some of the most talented and successful people have taught themselves. It's called D.I.Y. (do it yourself), and it takes practice, patience, and creativity. You've got all that, right? Right!

WORK TOGETHER

Yes, I know we just suggested that you do it yourself—but never underestimate the value of teamwork. Having a friend or group of friends who share your interests is so important—especially when times get tough. Collaboration can be very challenging, but it can also be incredibly rewarding—just ask us, the author and illustrator of this book. We keep each other motivated and focused, and even though we create most of our work by ourselves (Kate writes at home, and Miriam makes art in her studio), we are constantly sharing ideas and learning from each other.

MORE RAD GIRLS

One of the hardest parts about writing this book was deciding which stories to include—because there were just *so many*. It seemed like every day I would come across more stories of brave, bold, inspiring girls. There are tons of great stories of girls throughout history, and a literally never-ending supply of contemporary stories. This book could share a hundred, a thousand, or even ten thousand stories. We chose the fifty (well, technically forty-nine, until you write *yours*) stories in this book to get you started—but if you want to do some research on your own, check out these additional rad girls.

ADORA SVITAK (born in 1997) began writing stories when she was just four years old, and she published her first book at age seven. When Adora was twelve, she gave a powerful TED talk called "What Adults Can Learn from Kids." It's been viewed online more than four million times and has been translated into forty languages.

ALICE COACHMAN (born in 1922) was a track-and-field phenomenon born and raised in the segregated South. In 1948, she became the first African-American woman to win a gold medal when she competed in the high jump at the London Olympics. Many say she would have won more medals, but the 1940 and 1944 Olympics were cancelled because of World War II.

AMANI AL-KHATAHTBEH (born in 1992) is a writer, editor, and entrepreneur who founded the online magazine muslimgirl.com when she was just seventeen; it is now the #1 Muslim women's blog in the United States. Her memoir, *Muslim Girl: A Coming of Age* (Simon & Schuster, 2016), recalls her experiences of growing up Muslim after the events of September 11, 2001.

ANNA MAY WONG (born in 1905) is considered the first Asian-American movie star. She grew up in Los Angeles, fascinated by the movies being filmed there. She got her first part in a movie at age fourteen and her first leading role at seventeen. She acted for many years, and she often expressed frustration that her roles were stereotypical and offensive.

ANNIE MOORE (born in 1874) was the very first immigrant to pass through Ellis Island on the day it opened: January 1, 1892. That day was also Annie's seventeenth birthday; she had come to America from Ireland with her two younger brothers. A statue of Annie stands at Ellis Island today.

BETHANY HAMILTON (born in 1990) is a professional surfer who lost an arm in a shark attack when she was thirteen. Just one month after the attack, Bethany was back on her surfboard, teaching herself to swim, paddle, and surf with one arm. Three months after the attack, she entered her first professional competition, and she has gone on to win many awards.

CARMELA TEOLI (born in 1897) was the daughter of an Italian immigrant who worked in a dangerous Massachusetts textile mill alongside many other young girls. After a serious injury left her hospitalized for seven months, she was asked to testify before Congress by labor activist Margaret Sanger, who had organized a massive strike. Fourteen-year-old Carmela shocked lawmakers with a graphic account of her injury and how she was forced to drop out of school to work; it led to the passage of the Child Labor Law of 1913.

CAROLE KING (born in 1942) is one of the most successful songwriters of all time—and she began selling her songs to major music companies when she was a sixteen-year-old living in Queens, New York. She wrote the song "Will You Still Love Me Tomorrow?" when she was eighteen. It was first sung by the Shirelles, who made it the first-ever #1 hit by an all-girl group.

CHLOE AND HALLE BAILEY (born in 1998 and 2000, respectively) are sisters who perform together as Chloe x Halle. They started making music when they were eight and ten years old, when their dad taught them the basics of song structure. They started a YouTube channel, where they post videos of themselves covering popular R&B and pop songs. In 2013, they covered Beyoncé's song "Pretty Hurts," and it went so viral that Beyoncé herself shared it on Facebook—and then called the sisters to say how much she loved them. One year later, the sisters signed a major record deal with Beyoncé's record label.

CHLOE KIM (born in 2000) is an elite snowboarder who started riding at age four. She became the youngest person to win a gold medal at the winter X Games, when she was fourteen. And she won gold at both the Youth Olympic Games and the 2018 Olympic Games.

CLAUDETTE COLVIN (born in 1939) was an African-American teenager who refused to give up her seat on a segregated bus in Birmingham, Alabama, in March 1955. That day in school, Claudette had learned about black leaders like Sojourner Truth and Harriet Tubman, and she felt empowered. Claudette was arrested and sent to jail. Nine months later, in December, Rosa Parks refused to give up her bus seat in Montgomery, Alabama.

CLEOPATRA (born in 69 BCE) was the legendary Egyptian ruler who ascended to the throne at the age of seventeen. She was known for being brilliant, powerful, and strategic—and for speaking nine languages!

DEEPIKA KURUP (born in 1998) is an inventor, scientist, and clean-water advocate who invented an award-winning solar-powered water purifier when she was fourteen.

EDMONIA LEWIS (born in 1907) was a sculptor who began drawing and teaching herself to sculpt when she was a teenager. The daughter of a Native American (Chippewa) woman and an African-American father, she was orphaned at a young age and raised mostly by her mother's tribe. At fifteen she enrolled at Oberlin College, where she was one of the first black female students. She moved to Boston and then to Rome, where she had a successful career as a sculptor for over three decades.

THE EDMONSON SISTERS (Mary, born in 1832, and Emily, born in 1835) were African-American slaves who attempted to escape from slavery when they were teenagers. On April 15, 1848, when Mary was sixteen and Emily was thirteen, the brave sisters and seventy-seven other slaves snuck onto a ship called *The Pearl* that was headed north from Washington, DC, to New Jersey. They hid in boxes on the ship, and though they were caught, they went on to gain their freedom and become active in the anti-slavery movement.

ELINOR SMITH (born in 1911) was a pioneering aviator known as the "Flying Flapper." She learned to fly before the age of ten, made her first solo flight at fifteen, and became the youngest licensed pilot in the world at sixteen. At seventeen, she shocked her fellow pilots when she flew her plane under all four bridges over New York City's East River—because a male pilot had said there was no way she could do it!

ELLA FITZGERALD (born in 1917) is one of the most famous and beloved jazz singers of all time. She got her big break when she sang at amateur night at the Apollo Theater in New York City at age seventeen. She won first place (a $25 prize) and greatly impressed the audience.

That was huge for Ella, who'd spent several of her teenage years in a crowded orphanage.

ÉMILIENNE MOREAU-EVRARD (born in 1898) was a French war hero who helped to teach children and save lives during World War I. She was seventeen when Germany invaded France, and she started a school in her basement for local children, as well as a first-aid station for wounded soldiers.

EMMA WATSON (born in 1990), best known for her portrayal of Hermione in the *Harry Potter* movie series, is an outspoken feminist, actor, and human rights activist. She is a Goodwill Ambassador for the United Nations and helped launch the campaign HeForShe, which calls for men to work for gender equality alongside women.

EVA LEWIS (born in 1998) is an activist and artist from the south side of Chicago and cofounder of Youth for Black Lives, a Chicago-based youth activism organization focused on racial justice. During the summer of 2016, seventeen-year-old Eva and three of her friends organized a peaceful sit-in to protest police brutality and gun violence. More than a thousand youth showed up to peacefully make their voices heard.

HANNIE SCHAFT (born in 1920) is a famous Dutch resistance fighter, also known as "the girl with the red hair." From a young age, Hannie was interested in politics and committed to social justice. She was eighteen when World War II began, and when the Nazis started persecuting Dutch Jews, Hannie took action. Over the next several years, she worked in secret with other resistance fighters, including teenage sisters Freddie and Truus Oversteegen. They smuggled weapons and food, sabotaged Nazis, went on dangerous missions, and even took up arms in the effort to resist fascism. The Nazis placed Hannie on their "most wanted" list, and though she dyed her hair black, she was caught and executed in 1945.

HILDE KATE LYSIAK (born in 2006) is a young journalist who publishes her own local online newspaper, *Orange Street News*. She started it when she was eight, with the help of her dad. Hilde reports on the events in her town of Selinsgrove, Pennsylvania. She gained national attention when a murder occurred in her neighborhood and she was the first reporter on the scene.

IRÈNE JOLIOT-CURIE (born in 1897) was the daughter of the famed chemist Marie Curie. When she was eighteen, Irène joined her mother on the battlefields of World War II to help set up the mobile X-ray units that Marie had invented. She went on to become a famous scientist as well, and Irène and Marie are the only mother-daughter pair to both win the Nobel Prize.

JACKIE MITCHELL (born in 1913) was one of the first female pitchers in the history of professional baseball. She's known as "the girl who struck out Babe Ruth" because of her impressive performance during an exhibition game against the New York Yankees in 1931, when Jackie was seventeen. She also struck out Lou Gehrig!

JASILYN CHARGER (born in 1999) is a Native American teenager who is part of the resistance to the construction of the Keystone XL pipeline. She founded the International Indigenous Youth Council at Standing Rock and led her fellow Native American youth in standing up for their land, their people, and the health of the planet.

JESSICA WATSON (born in 1993) is the youngest person to sail solo, nonstop and unassisted, around the world. It took her 210 days, and she completed her journey in May 2010. She faced immense criticism and doubt from people who thought she was too young or not skilled enough to undertake such a dangerous voyage. But Jessica, who grew up sailing in Australia and lived on a boat with her family for many years, proved them wrong.

JOSEPHINE BAKER (born in 1906) was a movie star, performer, spy, and activist who began her performance career at fifteen, when the homeless teen was spotted dancing on the street and recruited to perform with a vaudeville troupe in St. Louis. She became a big hit, but she grew tired of the racism she experienced as a black performer. At nineteen, she headed to France, where she became Europe's biggest star.

JULES SPECTOR (born in 2001) is a feminist blogger and activist from New York City who runs the popular site teenfeminist.com, which she started when she was thirteen, seeking a way to speak up for girls about the issues that affect them. She has worked as a teen advisor for GirlUp! and writes regularly about feminism, politics, and the power of teenage voices.

KATIE LEDECKY (born in 1997) is a five-time Olympic gold medalist and fourteen-time world champion swimmer, the most in history for a woman. At fifteen, she was the youngest American to compete in the 2012 Summer Olympics. She won a gold medal and broke a major record. In the 2016 Summer Olympics, she broke the world record in the 800-meter freestyle event, beating her closest competitor by eleven seconds.

LIZ MURRAY (born in 1980) is an inspirational speaker and writer known for overcoming enormous odds when she went from being a homeless teenager to a top student at Harvard University. When Liz was fifteen, her mother died of AIDS, and her drug-addicted father couldn't pay the rent. He moved into a homeless shelter, and Liz took to the streets of New York City, sleeping in subway stations and stealing food. At seventeen, she made a vow to change her life and become a straight-A student. She studied hard and went to night classes, and eventually earned a full scholarship to Harvard. She has written a best-selling memoir, and her story was turned into a television movie, *Homeless to Harvard: The Liz Murray Story*.

LYNDA BLACKMON LOWERY (born in 1950) is a civil rights activist who, at age fifteen, was the youngest participant in the historic 1965 Selma civil rights march, a three-day voting-rights march from Selma to Montgomery, Alabama. It wasn't her first march—she was also present during the first attempt at a Selma-to-Montgomery march and was severely beaten by police on the infamous "Bloody Sunday" when she was just fourteen. Though traumatized and afraid, she wanted to try the march again to show that she could not be stopped.

MARI COPENY (born in 2007), from Flint, Michigan, has become known as "Little Miss Flint" for her role as a clean-water advocate and community leader. For several years, the water in Flint has been unsafe to drink; Mari watched friends get lead poisoning and her sister suffer terrible rashes from the tainted water. When she was eight, Mari wrote a letter to President Obama about the situation. He not only read the letter but also came to Flint to meet with members of the community— including Mari. Mari continues to use her voice to speak up about her beloved city and the health of its families.

MARIA MOZART (born in 1751) was the older sister of Wolfgang Amadeus Mozart, the famous composer. Maria was also a gifted musician; her father taught her to play the harpsichord when she was seven, and he took Maria and Wolfgang on tours to cities like Paris and Vienna. The siblings performed together for delighted audiences, and Maria often received top billing over her brother. However, once she became a teenager and was "of marrying age" she was no longer allowed to perform. She stayed at home with her mother while Wolfgang continued to tour Europe. There is some evidence that she composed music too and may even have helped her brother compose some of his best-known symphonies.

MARY, QUEEN OF SCOTS (born in 1542), also known as Mary Stuart or Mary I, is known for being crowned queen of two nations before she turned eighteen. She became the queen of Scotland when her father, James V, died when she was just six days old. At sixteen, she married the king of France, and she reigned as queen there until her husband died.

MIKAILA ULMER (born in 2005) is the founder of Me & the Bees, a company that makes lemonade sold at major supermarkets all over the United States. It began when Mikaila started a lemonade stand at age four, using her great-grandmother's special recipe from the 1940s. The beverage is sweetened with local honey, and it became so popular that Mikaila went on the television show *Shark Tank* when she was nine and pitched her business idea. She received an investment of $600,000 and was able to launch her own company. Mikaila is committed to saving honeybees, so she donates a percentage of her profits to organizations that work to save bees.

MONAE DAVIS (born in 2001) is a multi-sport athlete who became well known when she played in the 2014 Little League World Series—and pitched a shutout. She was the first African-American girl to play in the World Series, and she became the first Little League baseball player to be on the cover of *Sports Illustrated*. At thirteen years old, Monae could pitch a 70-mph fast ball. She also loves basketball, and her dream is to play in the WNBA.

NADIA COMĂNECI (born in 1961) is a Romanian gymnast who stunned the world when she became the first-ever gymnast to score a perfect 10 (she received a total of seven 10s as well as three gold medals). It was during the 1976 Olympics in Montreal, Canada, and the strong, energetic Nadia was just fourteen years old. She is credited with popularizing the sport of gymnastics around the world.

NINA MAE MCKINNEY (born in 1912) was one of the first African-American film stars in the United States. She debuted on Broadway in 1928 at age fifteen, when she danced as a chorus girl in the hit musical *Blackbirds of 1928*. A Hollywood film director noticed her performance and offered her a role in an upcoming film, making her the first African-American actress to hold a principal role in a mainstream film. She then signed a five-year contract with MGM, making her the first African-American actor to sign a contract with a major film studio.

OLIVIA BEE (born in 1994) is a photographer who began taking photography lessons when she was eleven. She experimented with the camera, mostly taking pictures of herself and her friends. She posted many of her images online, and when she was fourteen she was contacted by the Converse shoe company, who asked if she would take pictures for them. They featured her work in their ad campaigns, and her career took off from there. By eighteen, Olivia and her work had been featured in major magazines and newspapers, and she has taken pictures for Levi Strauss & Co., Adidas, and other major companies.

PARRIS GOEBELL (born in 1991) is an award-winning hip hop choreographer and dancer from New Zealand who got her start as a teenage hip hop dancer. She began taking hip hop dance lessons when she was ten, and at fifteen she put together an all-girl dance crew called ReQuest. They competed in major worldwide hip hop dance competitions, and by age twenty, Parris was doing choreography for Jennifer Lopez. She has worked with Janet Jackson, Rihanna, Nicki Minaj, Justin Bieber, and others.

POOJA NAGPAL (born in 1998) is a third-degree black belt in tae kwan do who started a nonprofit organization called For a Change, Defend, which aims to eliminate gender violence and empower women and young girls. Pooja has trained more than a thousand women and girls in Los Angeles, California—and in rural India as well. She helps girls develop strength and self-confidence, and she gives them the tools to defend themselves against violence and abuse.

PRETORIA SCHOOL GIRLS (founded in 2016) is a group of black high school students who, in 2016, bravely staged demonstrations to protest discriminatory policies about hair at their private school in Pretoria, South Africa. The girls were tired of being criticized and teased by teachers for having "messy" hair and often being told to "fix" their natural hair. They objected to the strict policies about proper hair maintenance that favored the hair of white students and was unfair to the styles worn by many black students (cornrows, braids, dreadlocks, Afros, and so on). The protest gained worldwide attention, with an online petition receiving twenty-five thousand signatures in just one day. Many of the girls were interviewed by global news organizations. The school apologized and changed its policies.

RUBY DORIS SMITH (born in 1942) was an activist and leader in the civil rights movement who began working with the Student Nonviolent Coordinating Committee (SNCC) when she was eighteen. When she applied to attend Spelman College, her letter of recommendation was written by Dr. Martin Luther King Jr.! Ruby helped organize countless nonviolent efforts, including lunch-counter sit-ins, Freedom Rides, boycotts, and voter registration drives. She spent more than a hundred days in jail for her tireless efforts and became the first female field secretary for the SNCC.

SEVERN CULLIS-SUZUKI (born in 1979) is a Canadian environmental activist who became known as "the girl who silenced the U.N. for 5 minutes" after she gave a powerful speech in front of United Nations delegates at the 1992 Earth Summit in Rio de Janeiro, Brazil. Twelve-year-old Severn spoke about the importance of environmental preservation, as well as the importance of listening to young people.

SONITA ALIZADEH (born in 1997) is a rapper from Afghanistan who uses her voice to speak out against child marriage. When Sonita was a teenager, her family fled from Afghanistan to Iran, where Sonita worked as a cleaning lady. She resisted the marriage her parents arranged for her, and, inspired by the American hip hop she'd begun listening to, wrote her own rap about being forced into marriage. A documentary filmmaker helped her make a music video, which went viral, bringing her message to people around the world.

SOPHIE SCHOLL (born in 1921) was a brave German teenager who resisted the Nazis and their leader, Adolf Hitler. Along with her brother and several friends, Sophie formed a secret activist group called the White Rose. They wrote powerful leaflets denouncing Hitler and were the first people in Germany to speak out against him. She was arrested for her actions, and at her trial she refused to apologize. She knew she had done the right thing for her country. She was executed when she was just twenty-one years old.

SYLVIA MENDEZ (born in 1936) was the daughter of Mexican and Puerto Rican immigrants. She was not allowed to attend the elementary school of her choice because of racist school segregation in California. In 1945, her family sued, along with several other Mexican families whose children had been denied the right to an education. Nine-year-old Sylvia bravely testified about her right to attend any public school, and the judge ruled in favor of the families. Sylvia became the first Mexican child to attend an all-white school in California.

TILLY SMITH (born in 1995) is credited with saving the lives of one hundred people in 2004 after she alerted them all to an approaching tsunami. Ten-year-old Tilly and her family were on a beach in Thailand when she noticed the warning signs of a tsunami: the tide went way out, the water began to bubble, and boats on the water bobbed up and down. Tilly had just studied tsunamis in her geography class; she

began alerting her parents and telling everyone to run to safety. The tsunami came minutes later, and no one who had heeded Tilly's warning was hurt.

THE WIDJEN SISTERS (Melati, born in 2001, and Isabel, born in 2003) live on the Indonesian island of Bali, where thousands of plastic bags wash ashore during Bali's annual wet season. After learning about global change-makers in school, and feeling inspired to make a difference in their own community, the sisters started Bye-Bye Plastic Bags in 2013, when they were just ten and twelve years old. Plastic pollution is a huge problem for the islands of Indonesia; the Widjen sisters' campaign sought to ban plastic bags from Bali. In 2016, after three years of hard work, the governor agreed to support their efforts to make Bali a plastic bag–free zone by 2018, with the rest of Indonesia to follow.

ZURIEL ODUWOLE (born in 2003) is a teenage filmmaker and education advocate who has traveled the world and interviewed the presidents and heads of state of twenty-four countries, talking to them all about the importance of girls' education. By age twelve, Zuriel had produced and edited four documentary films, all of which focus on the state of education in different African nations.

"Age is just a number. I started all the things that I'm doing now when I was nine. Just because you're young doesn't mean that you can't start taking action. If you have a dream, a goal, and a passion, all you have to do is set your mind to it and don't let anyone stop you."
—Zuriel Oduwole

RESEARCH AND RESOURCES

To do the research for this book, we relied on many different kinds of sources. We conducted interviews, read articles online, watched documentaries, and read books. Some of the girls and women featured in the book have been the subjects of books, films, and TV shows, and some have published memoirs and autobiographies. But since many of the stories in the book are very contemporary, we did rely a great deal on the internet for information. We checked the websites to make sure they were reliable, and we found multiple sources for each story. We also got to interview many of the contemporary young women in the book.

Some of our favorite sources for stories about rad girls are *Teen Vogue*, *A Mighty Girl*, *MAKERS*, the *Zinn Education Project*, and *Amy Poehler's Smart Girls*, as well as organizations like GirlUP, Girls Who Code, and Girls Inc.

To learn more about the girls and women featured in *Rad Girls Can*, check out these resources:

AMANDLA STENBERG: Watch Amandla in films like *The Hunger Games*; *Everything, Everything*; *Where Hands Touch*; and *The Hate U Give*. She is online at amandlastenberg.tumblr.com, and her comic, *Niobe: She Is Life*, is published by Stranger Comics.

ANN MAKOSINSKI: Find her on YouTube (@anastaire33), on social media (@annmakosinski), and at www.annmakosinski.com. Also check out www.googlesciencefair.com to see more amazing, innovative projects from young people around the globe.

ANNE FRANK: Anne's powerful, moving story is published as *The Diary of Anne Frank* (also known as *The Diary of a Young Girl*). There have also been numerous books, films, and television programs made about her story. The home in Amsterdam where Anne and her family hid is now a museum that preserves her work and legacy. Learn more at www.annefrank.org.

ARTEMISIA GENTILESCHI: Unfortunately, not much has been written about Artemisia, but she is honored in a famous art installation by Judy Chicago, *The Dinner Party*, which is a permanent display at the Brooklyn Art Museum.

ASHIMA SHIRAISHI: Ashima's book is called *How to Solve a Problem* (Random House, 2018). Videos of Ashima climbing and competing can be found online, and you can follow her on Instagram and Twitter at @ashimashiraishi.

BARBARA ROSE JOHNS: Barbara is one of many unsung heroines of the civil rights movement. There are no books or films about her, and despite her remarkable leadership, she is rarely mentioned in stories about school segregation and civil rights. Find more on a website devoted to her life and story, www.barbararosejohns.com.

CELESTE TINAJERO: Check out some of the environmental organizations that Celeste has worked with, including Alliance for Climate Action (acespace.org), the Brower Youth Awards (broweryouthawards.org), and Keep Truckee Meadows Beautiful (ktmb.org).

CLARESSA SHIELDS: *T-Rex: Her Fight for Gold* is a great documentary film about Claressa's life and boxing career. Videos of her fights, including her Olympic gold medal bouts, are all available online. She's on Twitter at @claressashields.

CLIMATE KIDS: Learn more about the Climate Kids lawsuit at www.ourchildrenstrust.org.

CONSTANCE MCMILLAN: In 2015, Constance was named one of the youth ambassadors for the Human Rights Campaign Foundation's Youth Well-Being Project. Check out the organization's work and learn more about their ambassadors at www.hrc.org.

EGYPT "IFY" UFELE: Check out Ify's fashions at www.chubiiline.com and on Instagram at @bullychasers.

ELIZABETH COTTEN: Some of the best recordings of Elizabeth's music were made in her bedroom on a reel-to-reel machine by folk singer Mike Seeger and released by Smithsonian Folkways. In 1984, at age ninety-one, Elizabeth won a Grammy for her album *Elizabeth Cotten Live* from Arhoolie Records.

EMMA TENAYUCA: *That's Not Fair!/¡No Es Justo!* (Wings Press, 2008) is a children's book about Emma written by poet Carmen Tafolla and Emma's niece Sharyll Teneyuca, and illustrated by Terry Ybáñez.

ESG: Their first album was a 1981 EP called *ESG*, and two years later they released a full-length album, *Come Away With ESG*, both on the record label 99. A compilation album called *A South Bronx Story* (Universal Sound, 2000) combines songs from both for a great introduction to the band.

HABEN GIRMA: Haben's website, www.habengirma.com, includes videos, articles, and a guide that Haben wrote for journalists with tips for writing positive disability stories.

HELEN KELLER: *The Miracle Worker* is a famous 1962 film about Helen Keller and Anne Sullivan; there have been several remakes, including one in 2000. Helen was a prolific writer and published twelve books during her lifetime. *The Story of My Life* is her classic autobiography, which she wrote at age twenty-two.

JANET MOCK: Janet is the author of two memoirs: *Redefining Realness* (Atria Books, 2014) and *Surpassing Certainty* (Atria Books, 2017). Learn more about her many projects at janetmock.com.

JAZZ JENNINGS: Jazz's television show, *I Am Jazz*, airs on TLC. The children's book that she cowrote when she was twelve is also called *I Am Jazz* (Dial Books, 2014). Her memoir is *Being Jazz: My Life as a (Transgender) Teen* (Crown Books for Young Readers, 2016).

JOAN OF ARC: This historical rad girl is the subject of multiple films, biopics, miniseries, and books.

KARTINI: Several collections of Kartini's writing and letters have been translated into English, including the book *Letters of a Javanese Princess* (W. W. Norton & Co., 1964). A feature-length film, *Kartini*, was released in Indonesia in 2017, but it is available only in Indonesian and does not have English subtitles.

LORDE: Find her website at lorde.co.nz and check out her YouTube channel, @LordeMusic.

LORELLA PRAELI: Some of the organizations Lorella has worked with include United We Dream (www.unitedwedream.org), the Anti-Defamation League (www.adl.org), and the American Civil Liberties Union (www.aclu.org).

MADISON KIMREY: Madison's blog is functionalhumanbeing.blogspot.com. You can watch videos of her many speeches on YouTube.

MALALA YOUSAFZAI: Malala's memoir, *I Am Malala: The Girl Who Stood Up for Education and Was Shot by the Taliban* (Little, Brown & Co.), was published in 2013. In 2017, she published a children's book called *Malala's Magic Pencil* (Little, Brown Books for Young Readers, 2017). Check out the film about her, *He Named Me Malala*. The diary she wrote for the BBC is still available online.

MARIA MITCHELL: The Maria Mitchell Association (mariamitchell.org) preserves Maria's legacy, which includes the Maria Mitchell Observatory on the island of Nantucket. One of her actual telescopes is on display at the Smithsonian National Museum of American History in Washington, DC.

MARLEY DIAS: Marley's first book is *Marley Dias Gets It Done: And So Can You!* (Scholastic, 2018). Read Marley's resource guide and database on her website at grassrootscommunityfoundation.org, and search the hashtag #1000blackgirlbooks on social media.

MARY SHELLEY: Two hundred years after its first publication, *Frankenstein* remains a classic work of literature, and the monster is an icon of film and TV culture around the world. Mary's other books are harder to find, but they include the novel *The Last Man*, written in 1826 and set far in the future, in the year 2100. Mary's mother was Mary Wollstonecraft, who wrote the foundational feminist philosophical text *A Vindication of the Rights of Woman* in 1792.

MARY BETH TINKER: Mary Beth travels around the country on her "Tinker Tour," educating young people about their First Amendment rights and activism. She's on Twitter at @marybtinker and online at tinkertourusa.org.

MARY-PAT HECTOR: Mary-Pat's website is marypathector.com, and she works with the organization National Action Network (nationalactionnetwork.net).

MEMORY BANDA: Memory has worked closely with Girls Empowerment Network Malawi (www.genetmalawi.org) and Let Girls Lead (www.riseuptogether.org). Her TED talk can be found online, and she's on Twitter at @memorybanda75.

MISTY COPELAND: The best way to experience Misty Copeland is to see her perform live at the ballet—but if that's not possible, you can watch footage of her dancing online. Her memoir is called *Life in Motion: An Unlikely Ballerina* (Touchstone, 2015), and she also wrote a children's book, *Firebird* (G. P. Putnam's Sons Books for Young Readers, 2014). Her website is www.mistycopeland.com.

MUSLIM GIRLS MAKING CHANGE: Find out more and watch videos of their performances at muslimgirlsmakingchange.weebly.com.

PHIONA MUTESI: *The Queen of Katwe: A Story of Life, Chess, and One Extraordinary Girl's Dream of Becoming a Grandmaster* by Tim Crothers (Scribner, 2012) chronicles Phiona's life. It was turned into a movie, *The Queen of Katwe*, released by Disney in 2016.

RADICAL MONARCHS: The *Guardian* newspaper made a twenty-minute documentary called *Radical Brownies*, which can be found online. Learn more about the Monarchs at their website, radicalmonarchs.org.

RUBY BRIDGES: Ruby has written several books for young readers that tell her story, including *Ruby Bridges Goes to School: My True Story* (Scholastic, 2009). *The Story of Ruby Bridges* (Scholastic, 1995) was written by Robert Coles, a child psychiatrist who volunteered to help support Ruby while she was in school. In 1998, Disney made a feature-length film called *Ruby Bridges*.

THE SCHIMMEL SISTERS: *Off the Rez* is a documentary film about the Schimmel sisters and their lives on and off the reservation. Watch lots of footage of Shoni and Jude playing ball by searching their names on YouTube.

S. E. HINTON: S. E. Hinton's five young adult novels are *The Outsiders* (Viking, 1967), *That Was Then, This Is Now* (Viking, 1971), *Rumble Fish* (Viking, 1975), *Tex* (Viking, 1979), and *Taming the Star Runner* (Dell, 1988). Her website is www.sehinton.com, and she's on Twitter at @se4realhinton.

SELENA: Selena released five successful solo albums in the six years before she died, including *Amor Prohibido* (1994) and *Dreaming of You* (released posthumously in 1995). Some of her most popular songs are "Como la Flor," "Bidi Bidi Bom Bom," and "Dreaming of You." A 1995 film about her life, *Selena*, starred a young Jennifer Lopez.

SKY BROWN: Sky (and her little brother, Ocean) are all over social media—check out their skating and surfing adventures on YouTube (@awsmkids) and Instagram (@awsmkids).

SOPHIE CRUZ: Watch Sophie's speech at the Women's March on YouTube. To learn more about how to support immigrant families like Sophie's, check out www.fwd.us and fightforfamilies.org.

TAVI GEVINSON: *Rookie* can be found online at rookiemag.com. Tavi has also edited the book series *Rookie Yearbook* (Razorbill, 2014), and her original blog still lives at thestylerookie.com.

TRISHA PRABHU: The ReThink app can be found in the Apple and Android app stores and at rethinkwords.com. Trisha's website is trishaprabhu.com, which is where you can see her TED talks *and* footage of her appearances on the TV show *Shark Tank*.

YUSRA MARDINI: Yusra works with the United Nations Refugee Agency, also known as the UNHCR (www.unhcr.org).

GRATITUDE

Thank you, thank you, thank you to the rad Ten Speed team. We're so glad to live close by, and so glad that you don't (seem to) mind our popping by for tea, edits, and brainstorming sessions. Biggest thanks to Julie Bennett, Ashley Pierce, Natalie Mulford, Windy Dorresteyn, Emma Campion, Serena Sigona, and the super-raddest designer, Lizzie Allen.

To our supremely rad agents, Charlotte Sheedy and Steven Malk.

Endless gratitude to our friends, family members, neighbors, and colleagues who support, encourage, and inspire us! Special thanks to Aya de Leon, Carolina de Robertis, Caroline Paul, Casey Orr, Charlie Stuip, Chiara Barzini, Dunstan Bruce, Jason Pontius, Dr. Larissa Mercado-Lopez, Lena Wolff, Leslie van Every, Lisa Brown, Megan Gordon, Melissa and W. Kamau Bell, Michelle Tea, Nikki McClure, Sarah Sophie Flicker, the Solidarity Sundays crew, Tara Jepsen, Thomas Page McBee, and Will Schwartz.

When you're an artist *and* a parent, childcare is essential—thanks to the grandparents, friends, caregivers, and teachers who kept our kids safe and entertained while we made this book, including Ace Morgan, Barbara and Doug Schatz, Daniela Sea, Duff McGee, Gabe Winer, Jenny Bergrenn and Jim Briggs, Judi Bertolin, Julia Beers, Kim Robinson, Linda Carr and the Arts and Humanities Academy, Lisa Kelly, Nana, the folks at Oakland Kajukenbo, Ruby Sullivan, Stella Burke, Tammy Rae Carland, and Terri Fashing.

Thank you to the many educators, librarians, and booksellers who support our work.

And finally, such special thank-yous to all the rad girls (and parents and managers and agents of rad girls) who agreed to be interviewed for this book, or who took time to review stories and illustrations and offer feedback. It was so much fun getting to know you all!

Amandla Stenberg and Brett Ruttenberg

Anayvette Martinez and the Radical Monarchs

Ann Makosinski and Nan Fisher

Ashima Shiraishi and Austin Turner

Celeste Tinajero

Claressa Shields and Jamie Fritz

Cordelia and Jennifer Longo

Egypt and Dr. Reba Renee Perry-Ufele

Haben Girma

Hawa Adam and Kiran Waquar

Hazel and Margo Van Ummersen

Janet Mock and Lauren Glover

Julia Olson, Lillian Garcia, and Meg Ward at Our Children's Trust

Lorella Praeli

Madison Kimrey

Marley and Janice Johnson Dias

Mary-Pat Hector

Mary Beth Tinker

Misty Copeland and Gilda Squire

Sky and Stu Brown

Trisha and Bhanu Prabhu

Yusra Mardini and Niclas Schmoll

ABOUT THE AUTHOR AND ILLUSTRATOR

Kate Schatz and Miriam Klein Stahl are the author and illustrator of the *New York Times* best-selling books *Rad American Women A–Z* and *Rad Women Worldwide*, and of *My Rad Life: A Journal.* They live in the San Francisco Bay Area with their families and pets (Kate has a husband, two kids, and three cats; Miriam has a wife, a daughter, and a dog). Kate and Miriam are artists, educators, and activists who dream of and work toward a just, feminist, and rad future for all.

Miriam's papercut illustrations are created using paper, pencil, and an X-Acto knife.

Learn more at www.radgirlscan.com.

KATE SCHATZ, AGE 7

MIRIAM KLEIN STAHL, AGE 7

INDEX

RAD GIRLS CAN ACT LEARN CREATE PLAY WIN LEAD S
CHANGE LOVE INNOVATE RIDE INVENT DANCE TRANSFO
WONDER ACHIEVE LEARN CREATE PLAY WIN LEAD SPEA
LOVE INNOVATE RIDE INVENT DANCE ACT TRANSFORM
ACHIEVE DANCE TRANSFORM LISTEN SCORE CLIMB
LEARN CREATE PLAY WIN LEAD SPEAK SING RUN WRIT
RIDE INVENT DANCE SCORE CLIMB SURVIVE SKATE
LISTEN SCORE CLIMB SURVIVE SKATE WORK PERFOR
SPEAK SING RUN WRITE DREAM TRANSFORM LISTEN S
ACHIEVE LEARN CREATE ACT PLAY WIN LEAD SPEAK SI
INNOVATE RIDE INVENT DANCE TRANSFORM LISTEN SC
LISTEN ACHIEVE DANCE TRANSFORM CHANGE FIGHT
RIDE INVENT DANCE TRANSFORM LISTEN SCORE ACT
DREAM COMPETE FIGHT CARE CHANGE LOVE INNOVAT
SURVIVE SKATE WORK PERFORM WONDER ACHIEVE D
WORK PERFORM WONDER ACHIEVE LEARN CREATE PLA
ACHIEVE LEARN CREATE ACT PLAY WIN LEAD SPEAK